THIS BOOK BELONGS TO:

Welcome To
THE MUSHROOM BOOK

Thank you for supporting Studio 825

Enjoy the 35 hand drawn illustrations
as they take you through some of the
fascinating fungus of the world

Finished Coloring?

Share your pages with us using our hashtags:
#studio825 #colorstudio825 #studio825coloringbook

Check out the Studio 825 Social Media

www.studio825vibe.com

Questions? Contacts Us: contact@studio825vibe.com

COLOR TEST

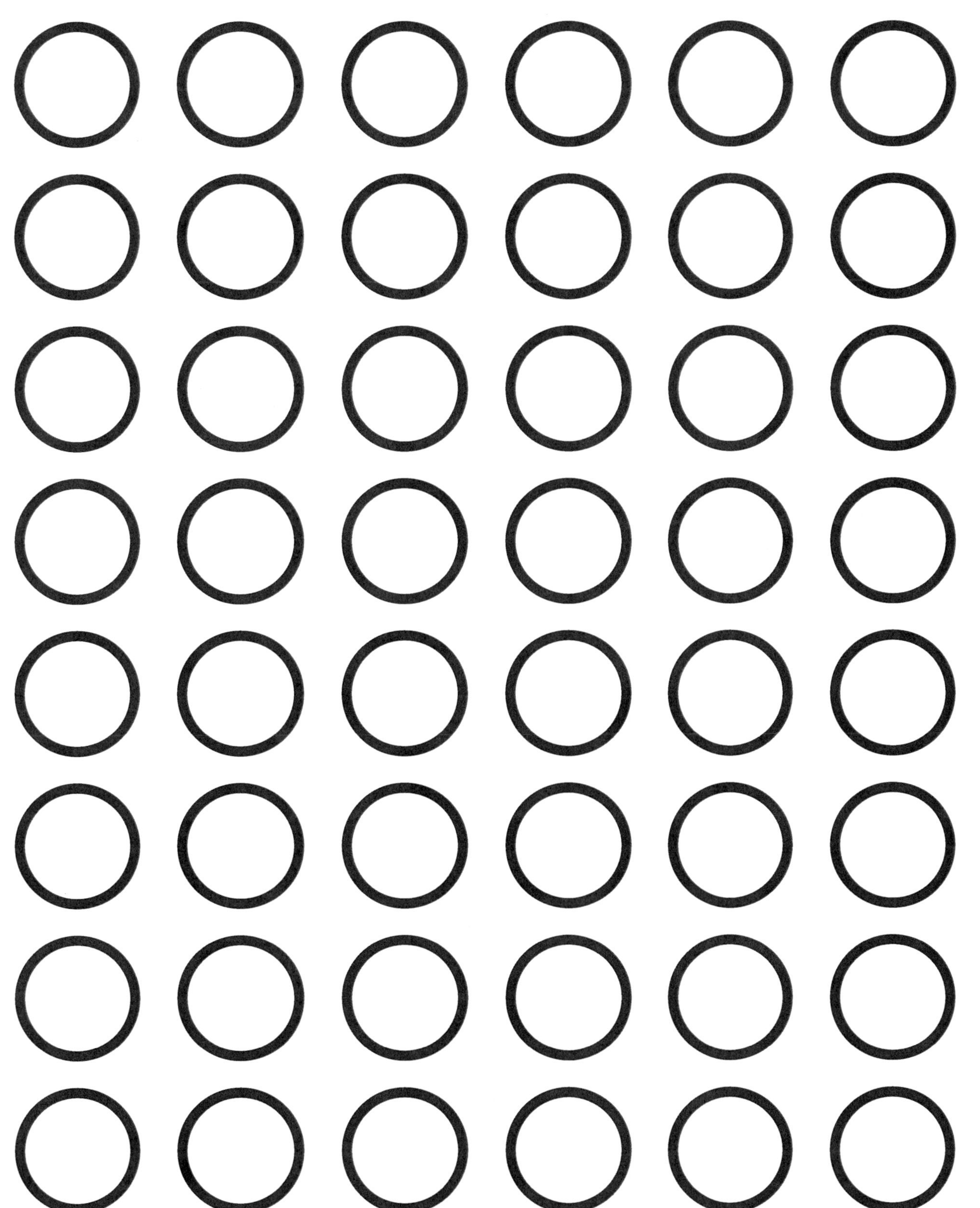

WITCHES CAP
Hygrocybe conica

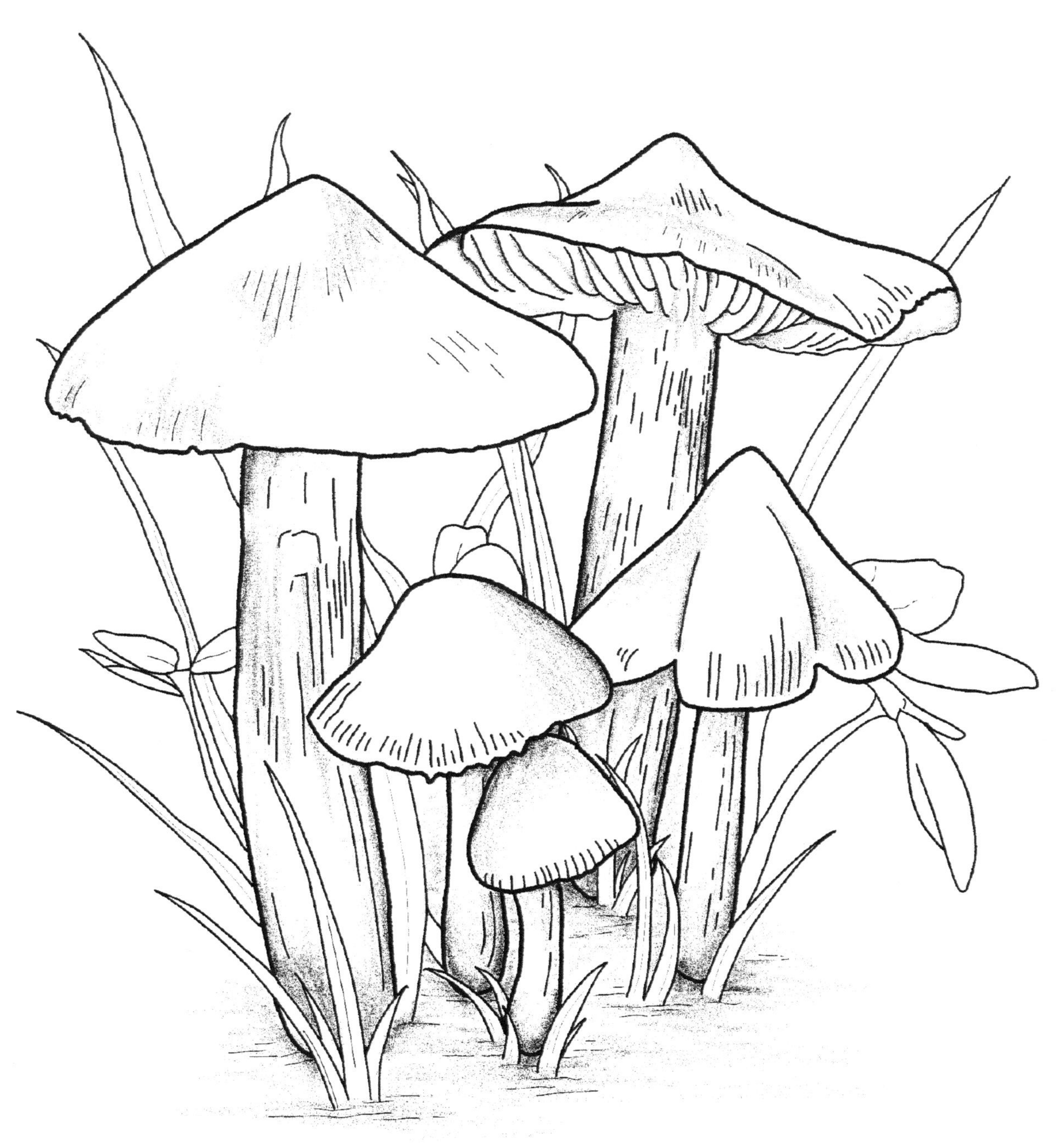

COMMON MOREL
Morchella esculenta

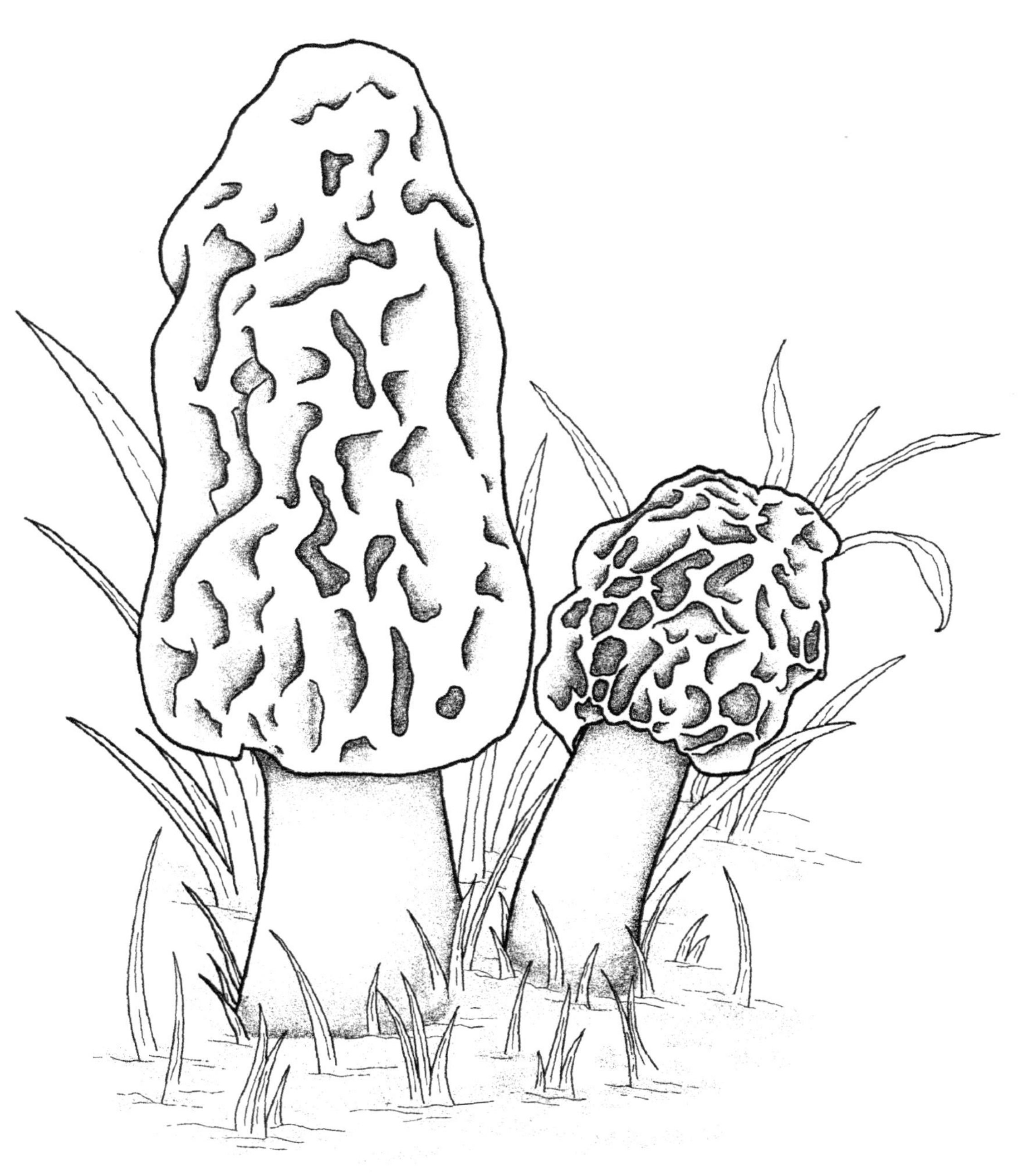

SCARLET ELF CUP
Sarcoscypha coccinea

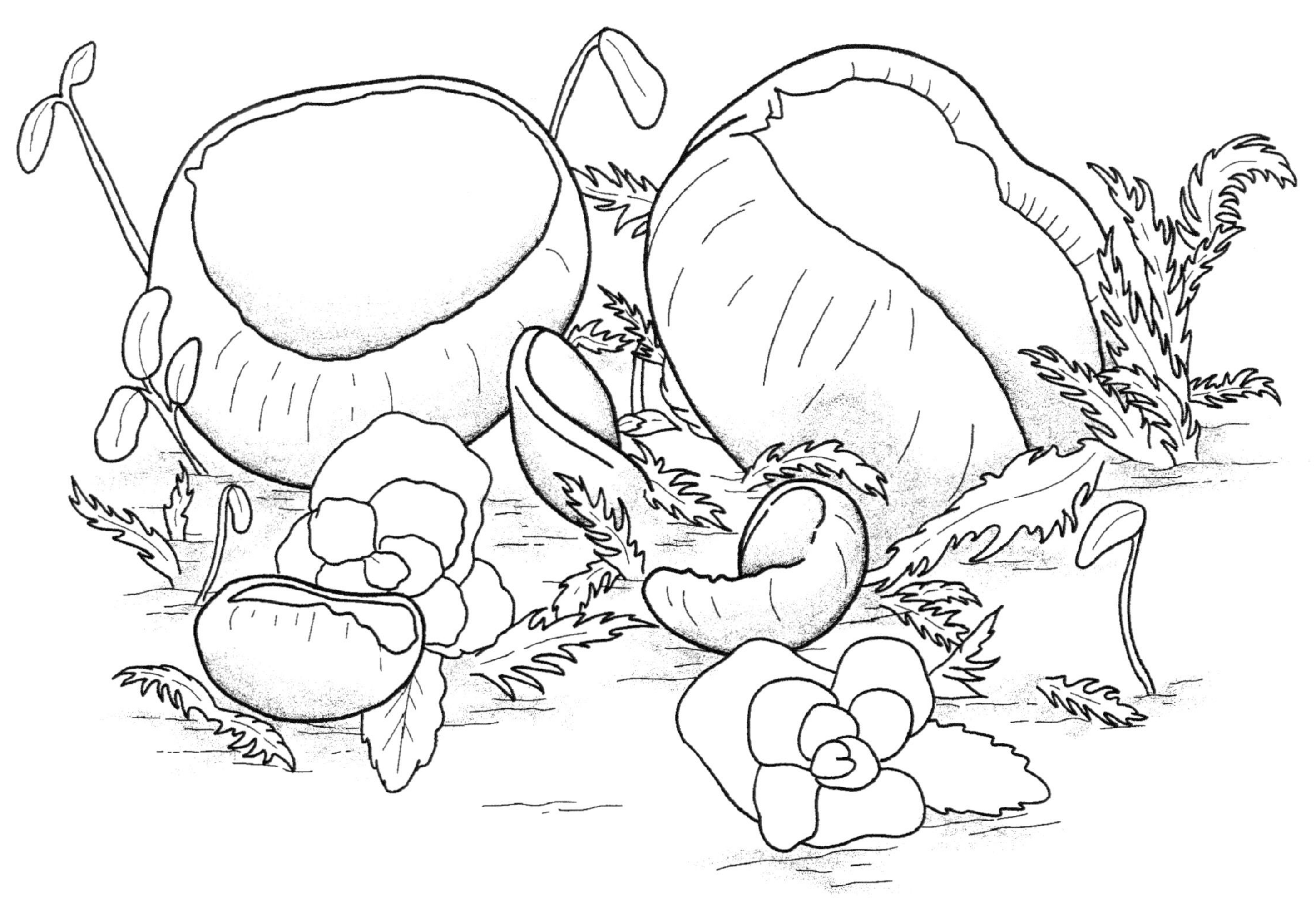

DEATH CAP
Amanita phalloides

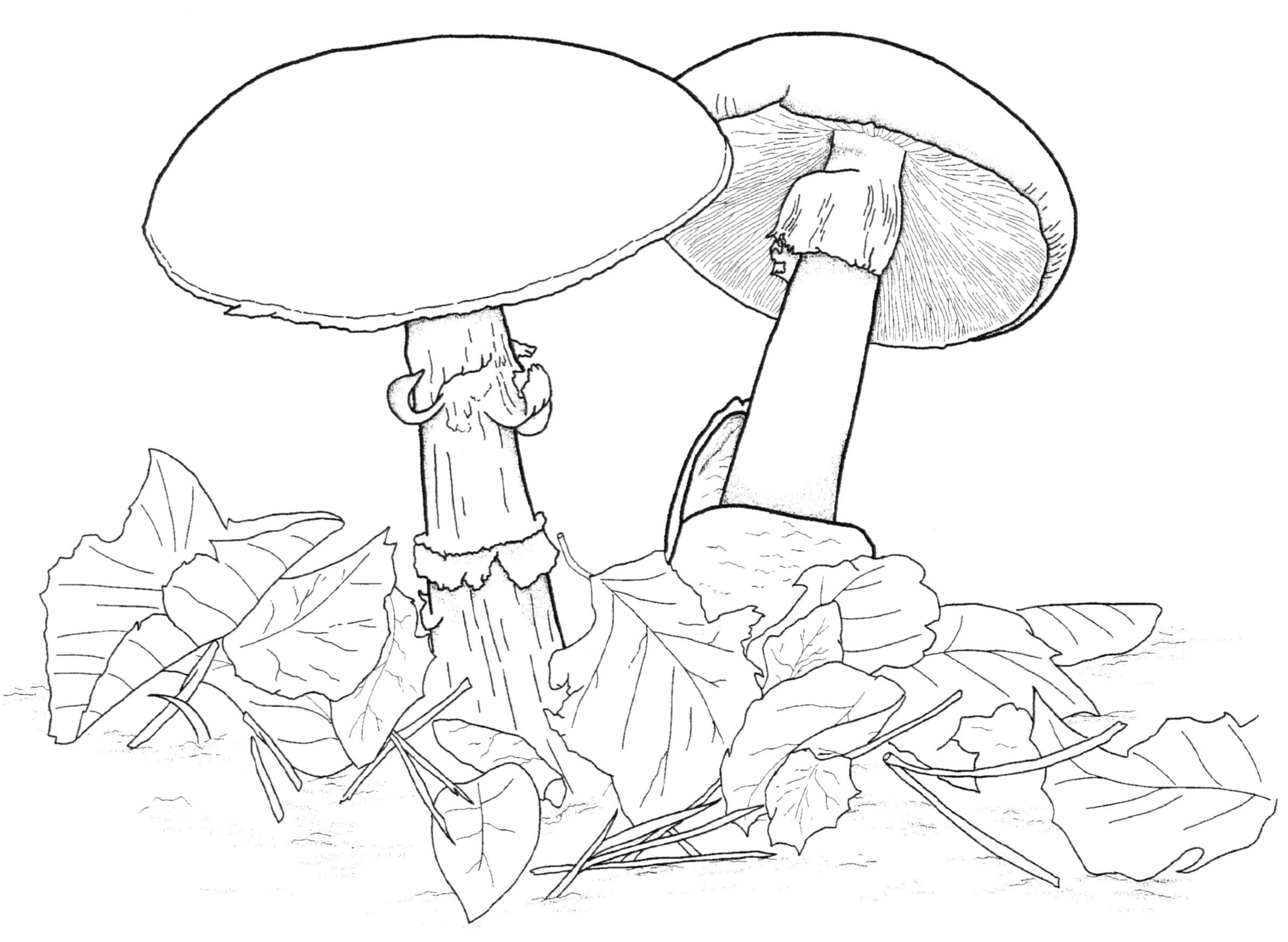

CHICKEN OF THE WOODS
Laetiporus

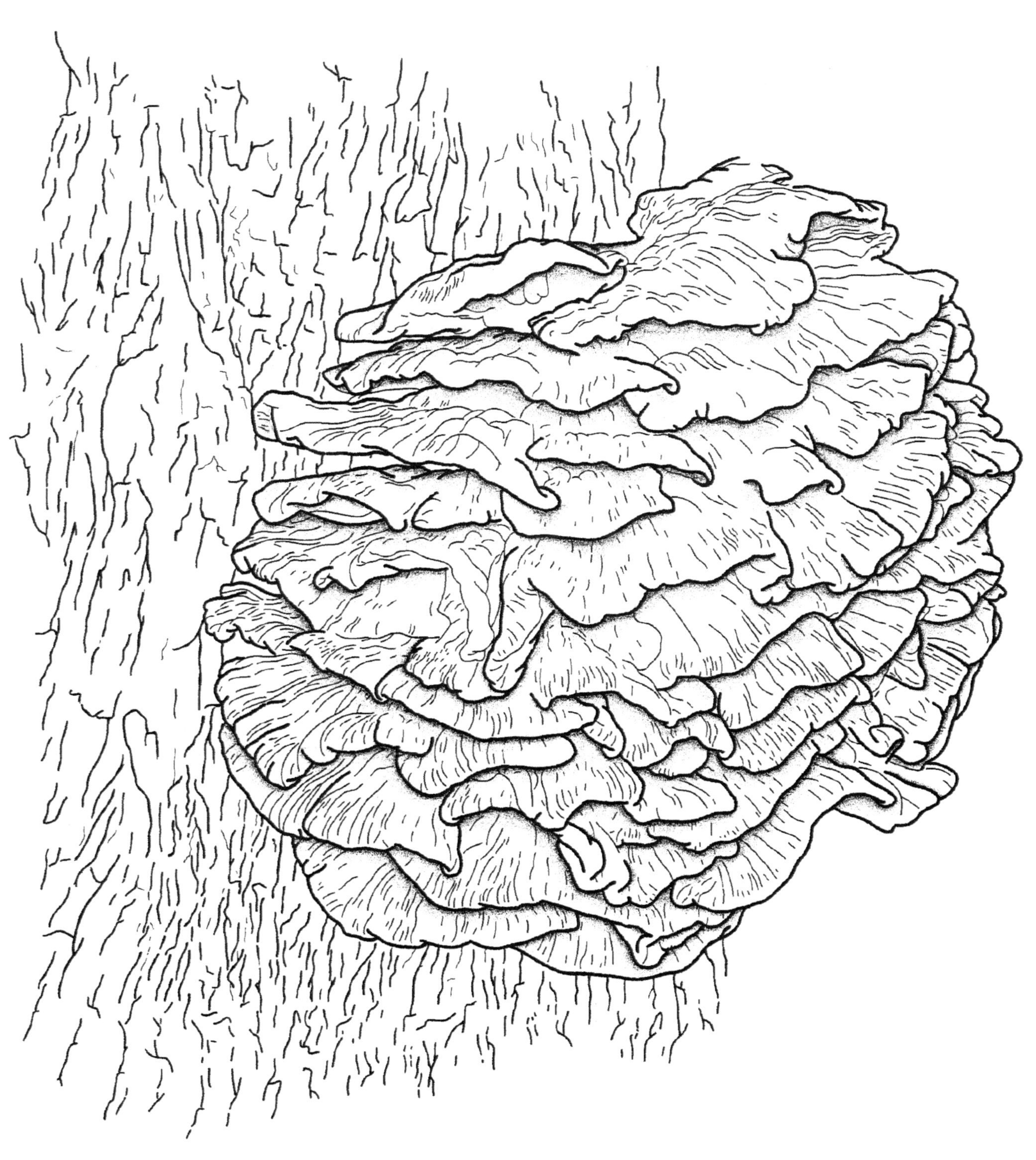

CESAR'S MUSHROOM
Amanita caesarea

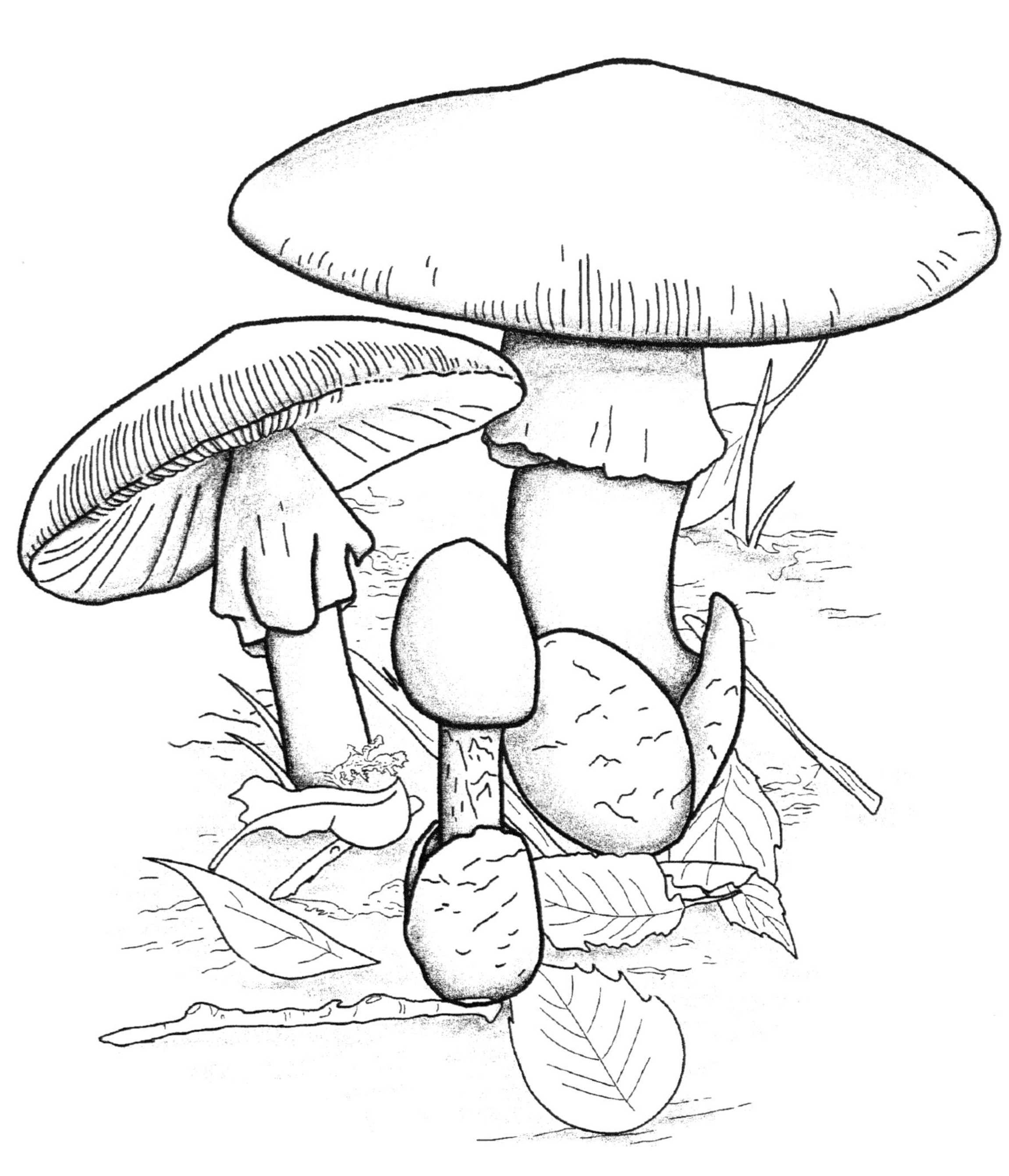

JELLY BABY
Leotia lubrica

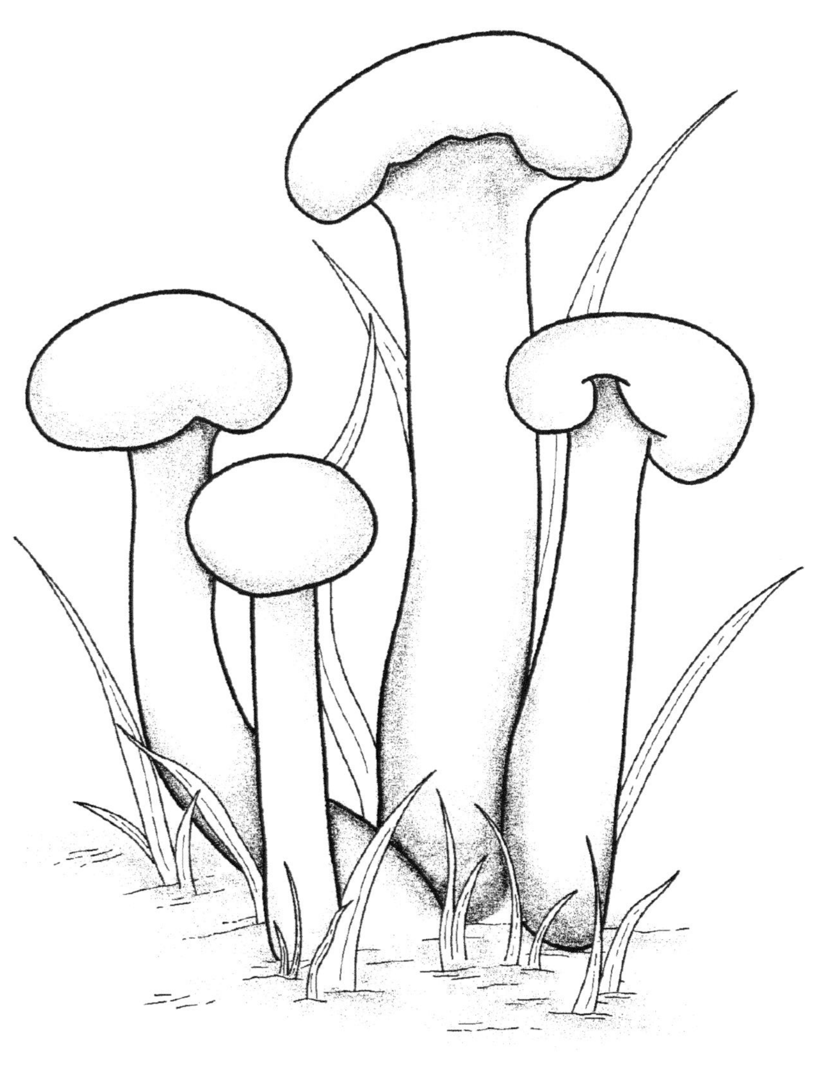

SALMON PINKGILL

Entoloma quadratum

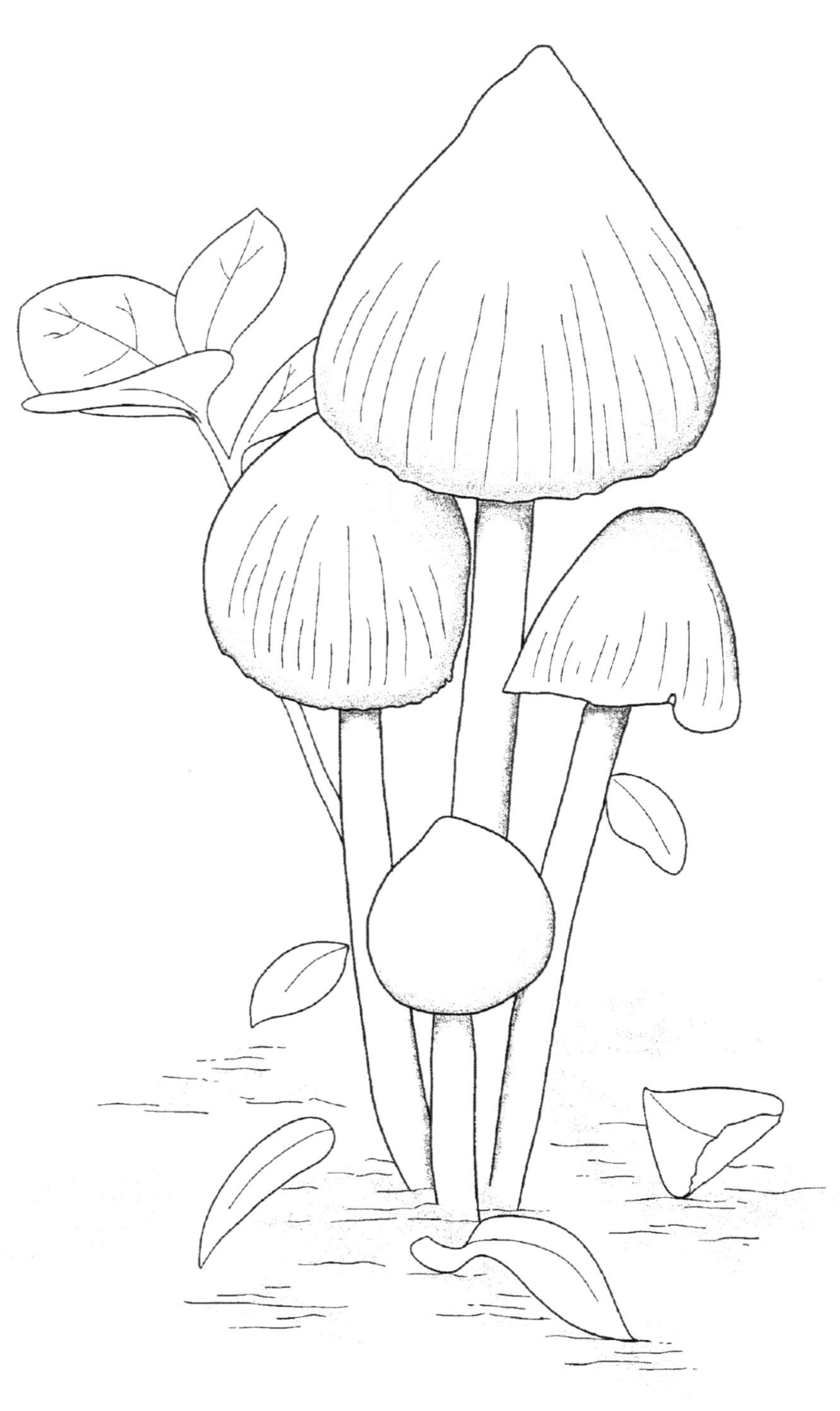

VIOLET CORAL

Clavaria zollingeri

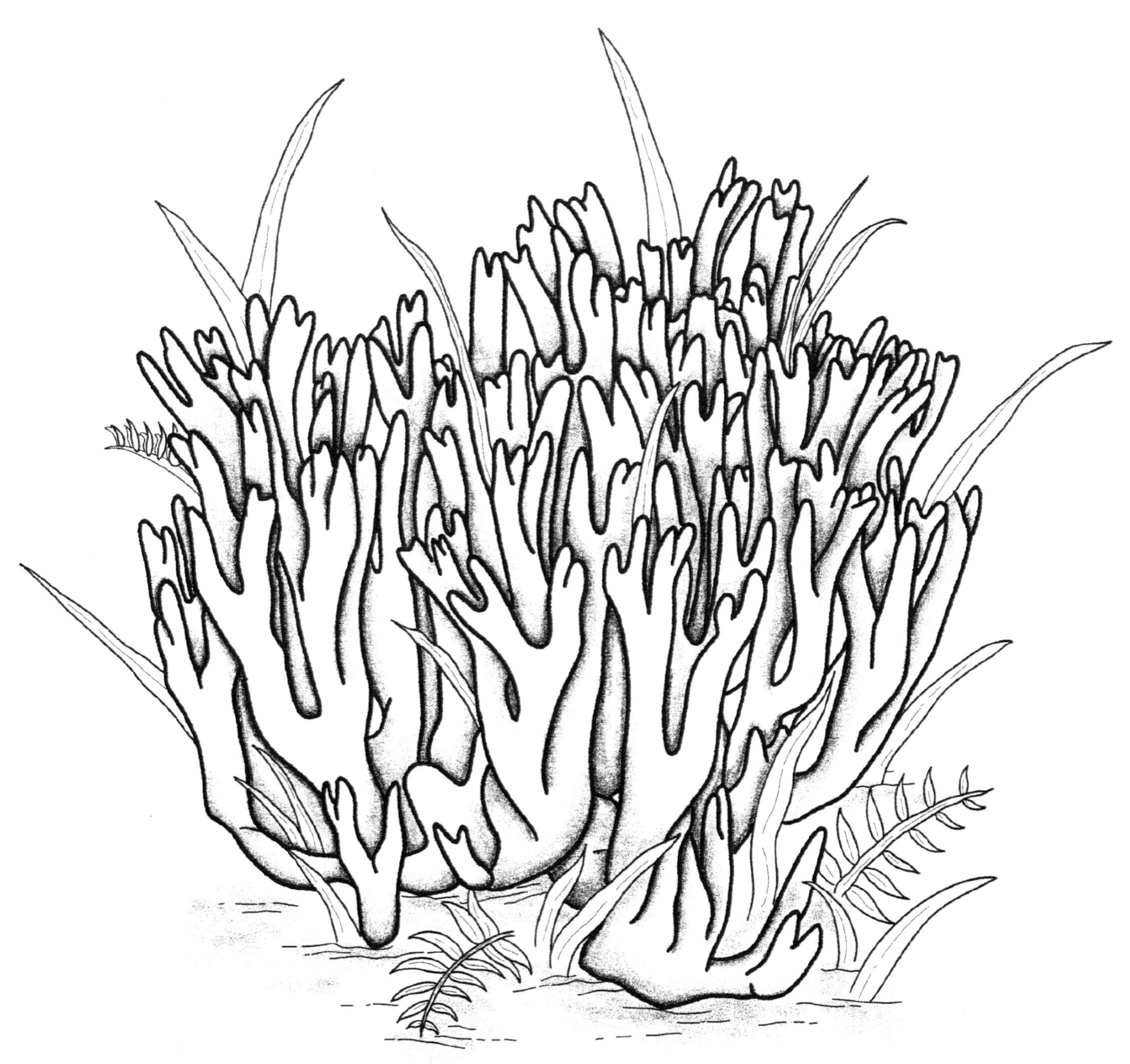

FLY AGARIC
Amanita muscaria

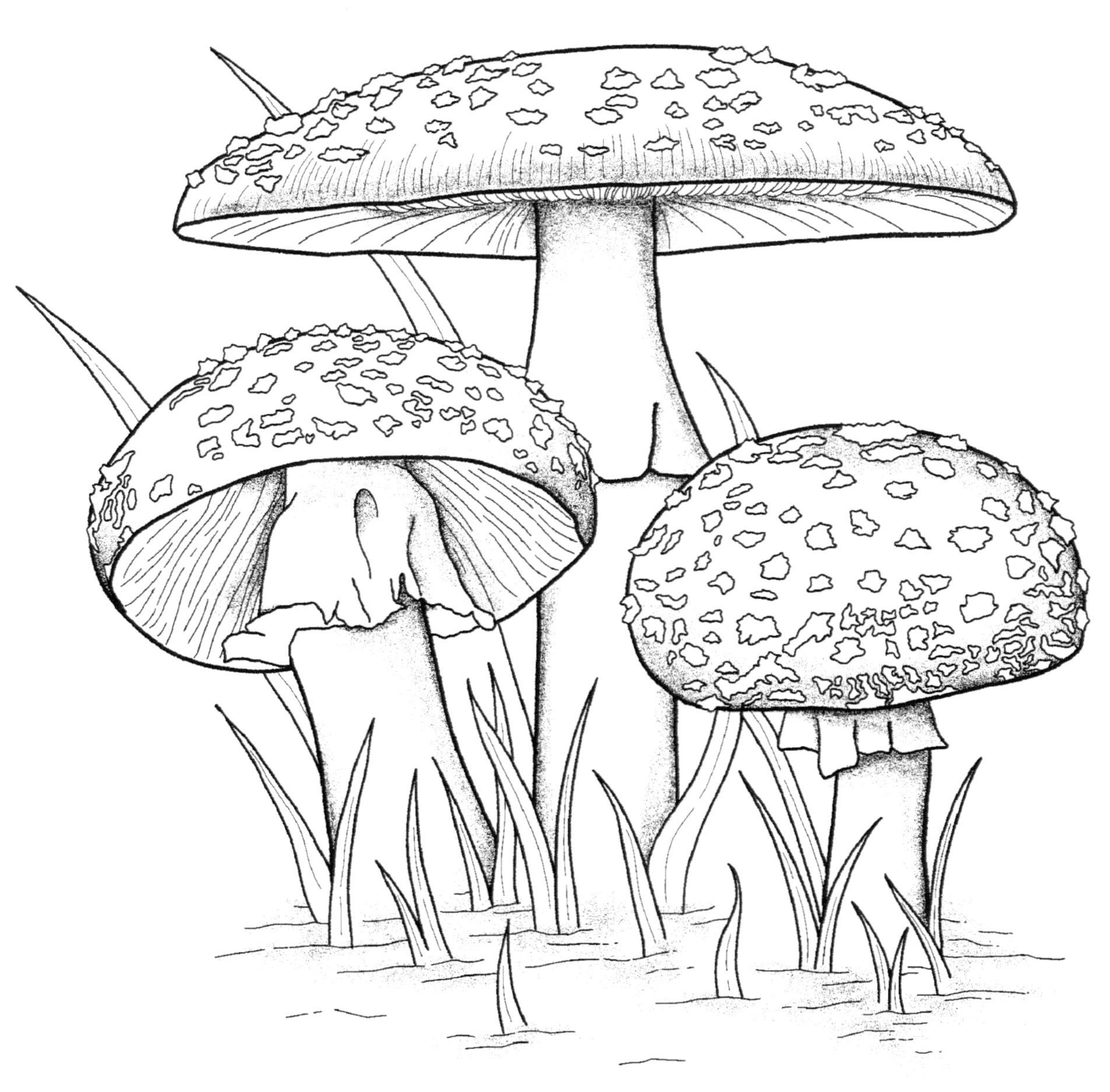

KING BOLETE

Boletus edulis

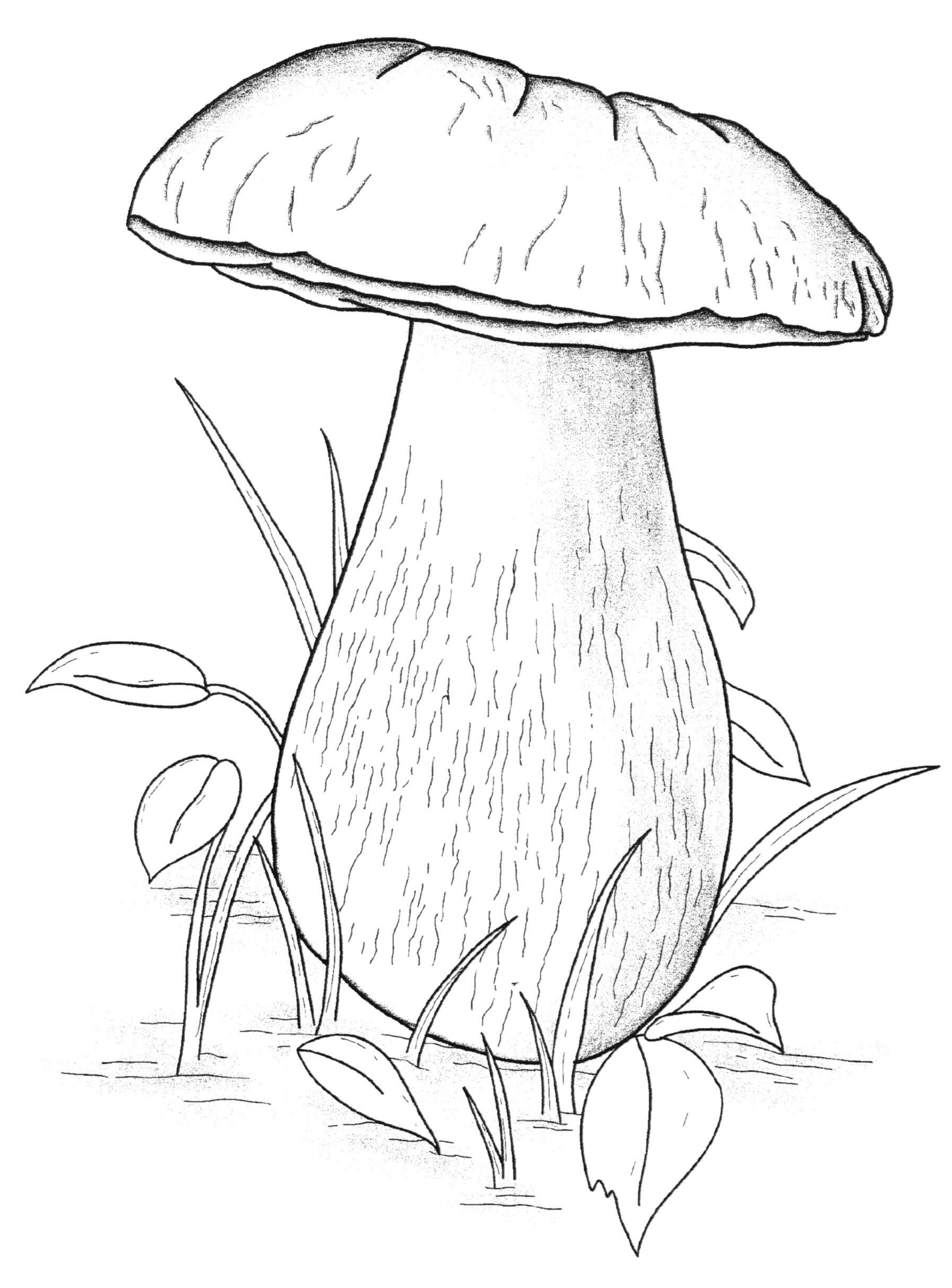

BLUE CHANTARELLE
Polyozellus

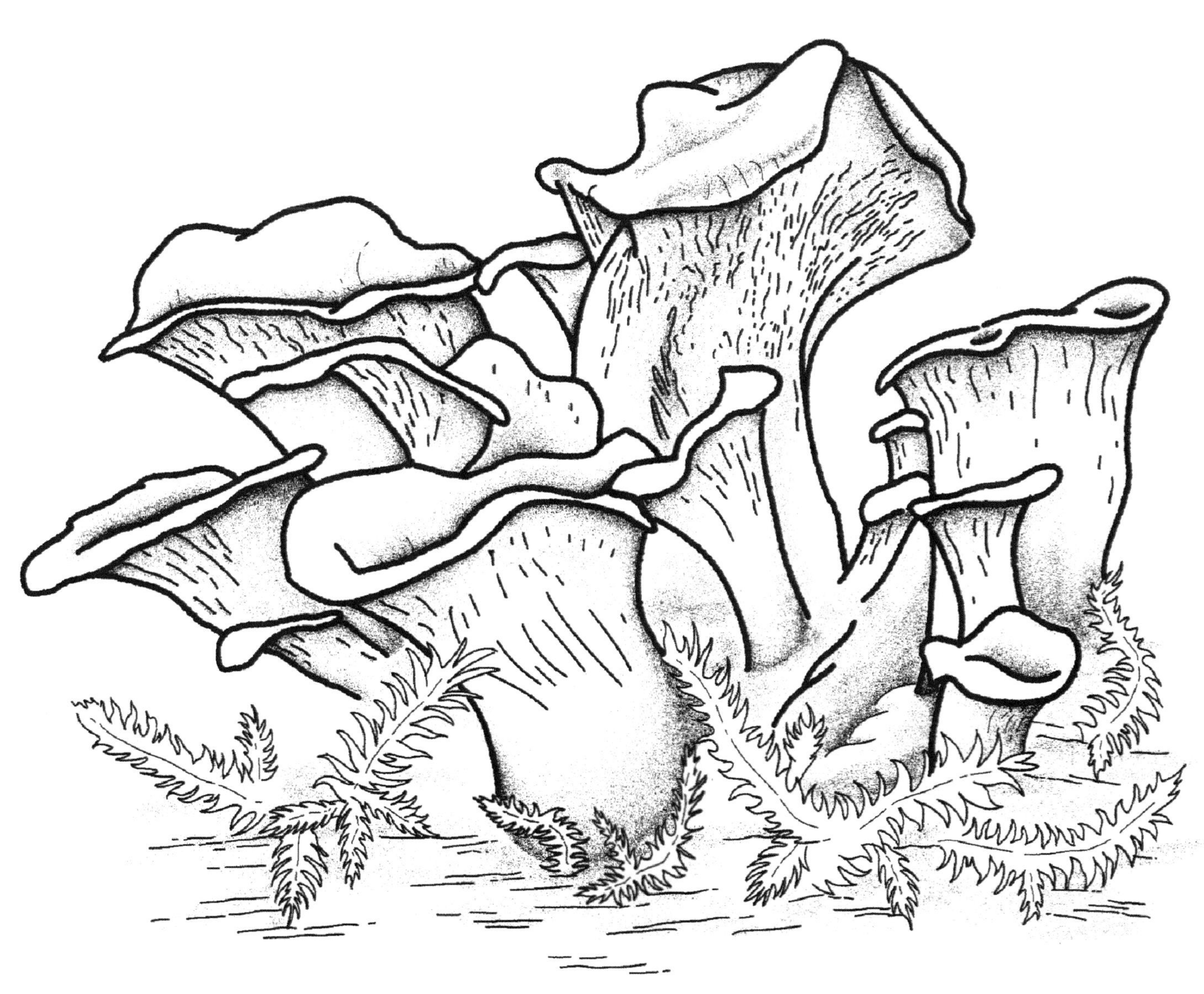

CANDY CAP
Lactarius camphoratus

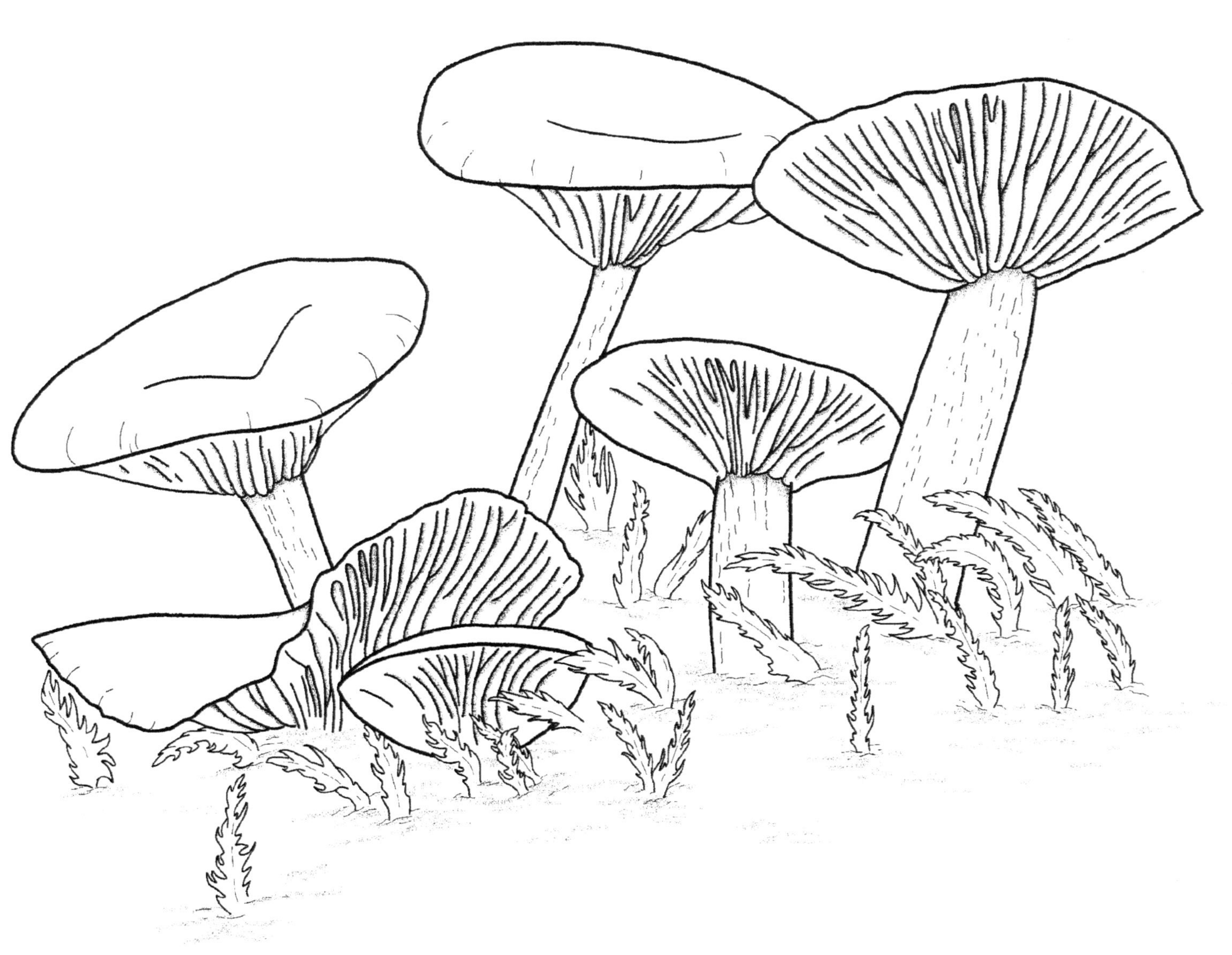

WITCHES CAULDRON
Sarcosoma globosum

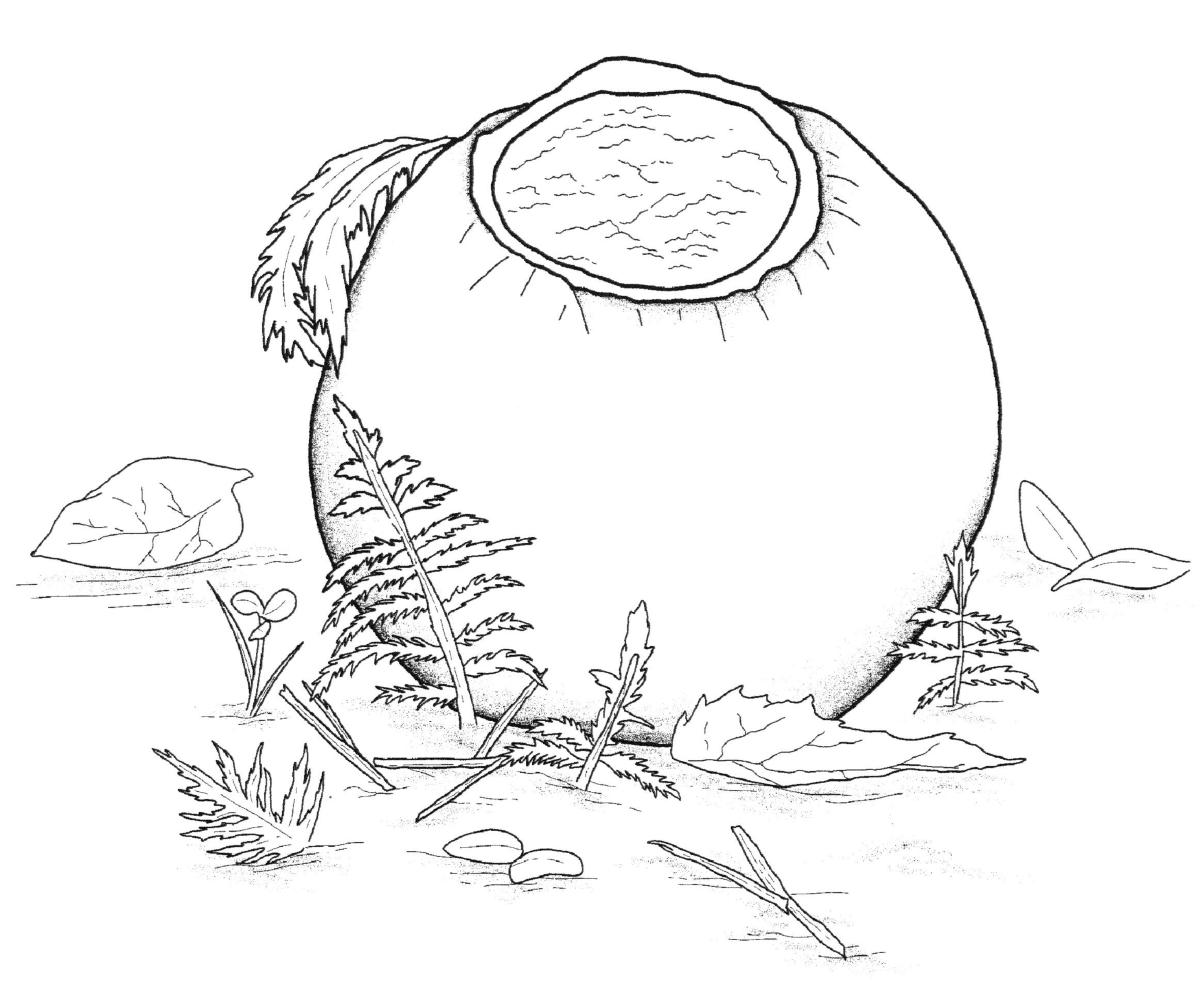

FAIRY FAN
Spathularia flavida

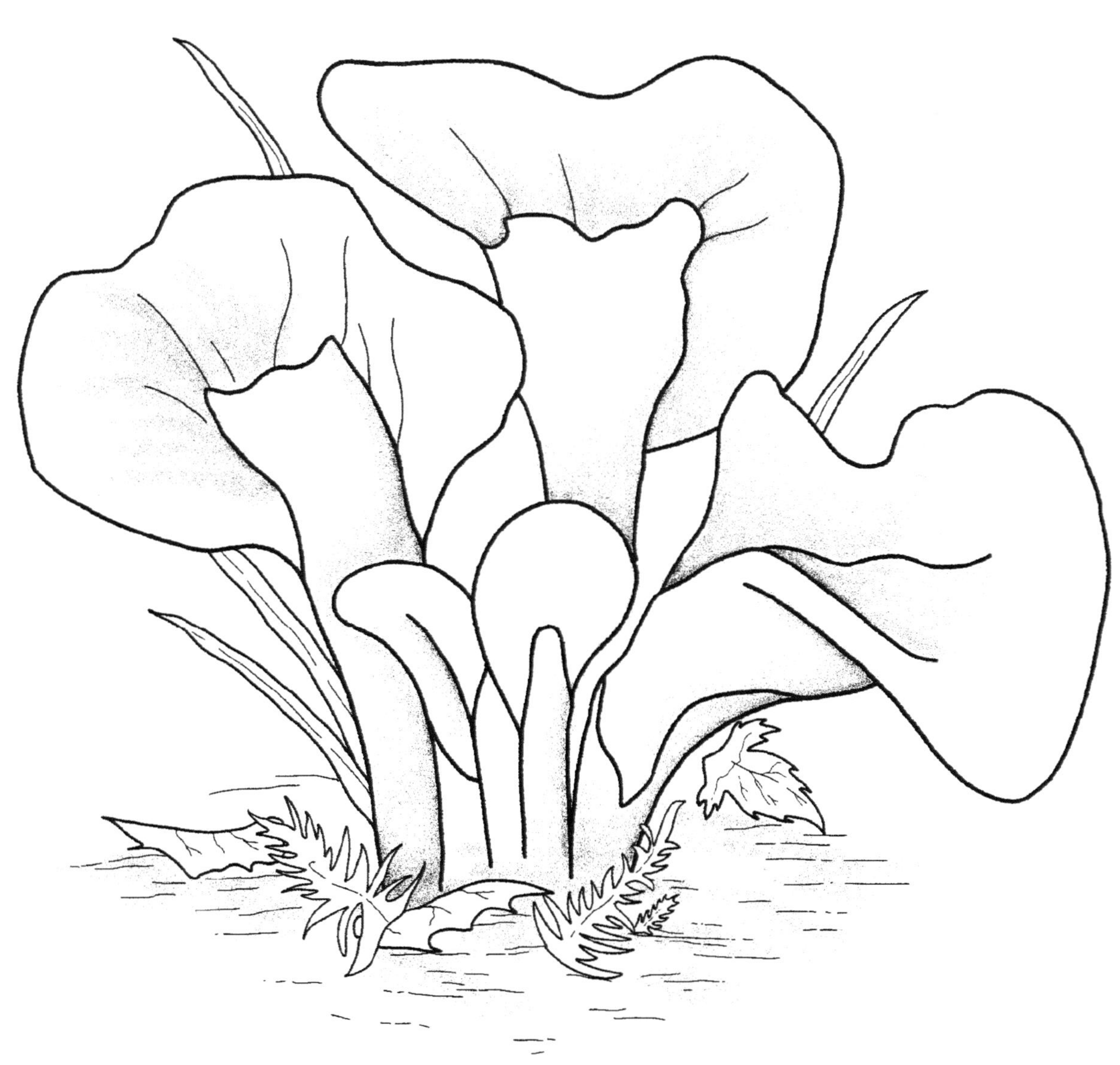

WOOD BLEWIT

Clitocybe nuda

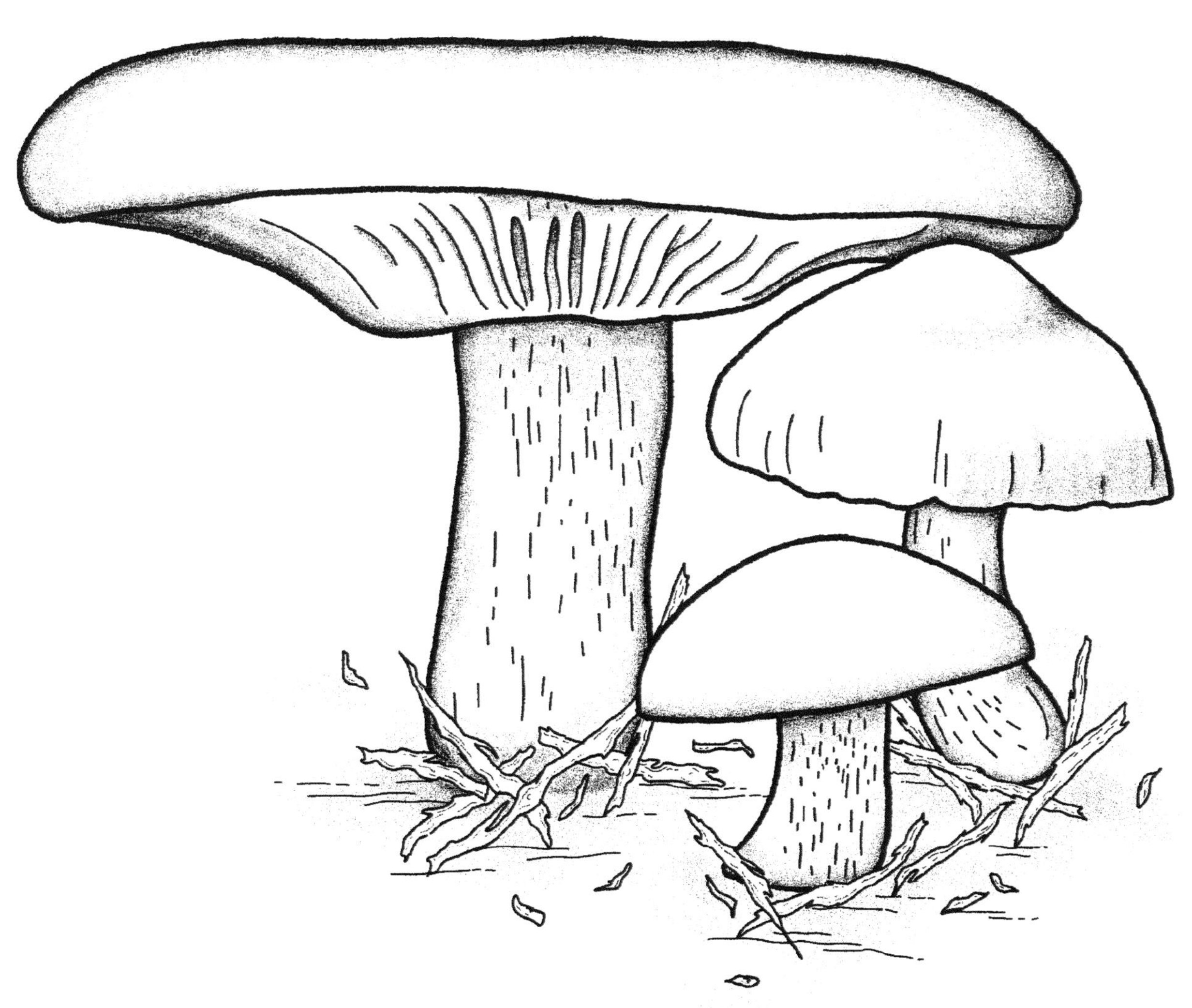

PINE CONE CAP
Strobilurus tenacellus

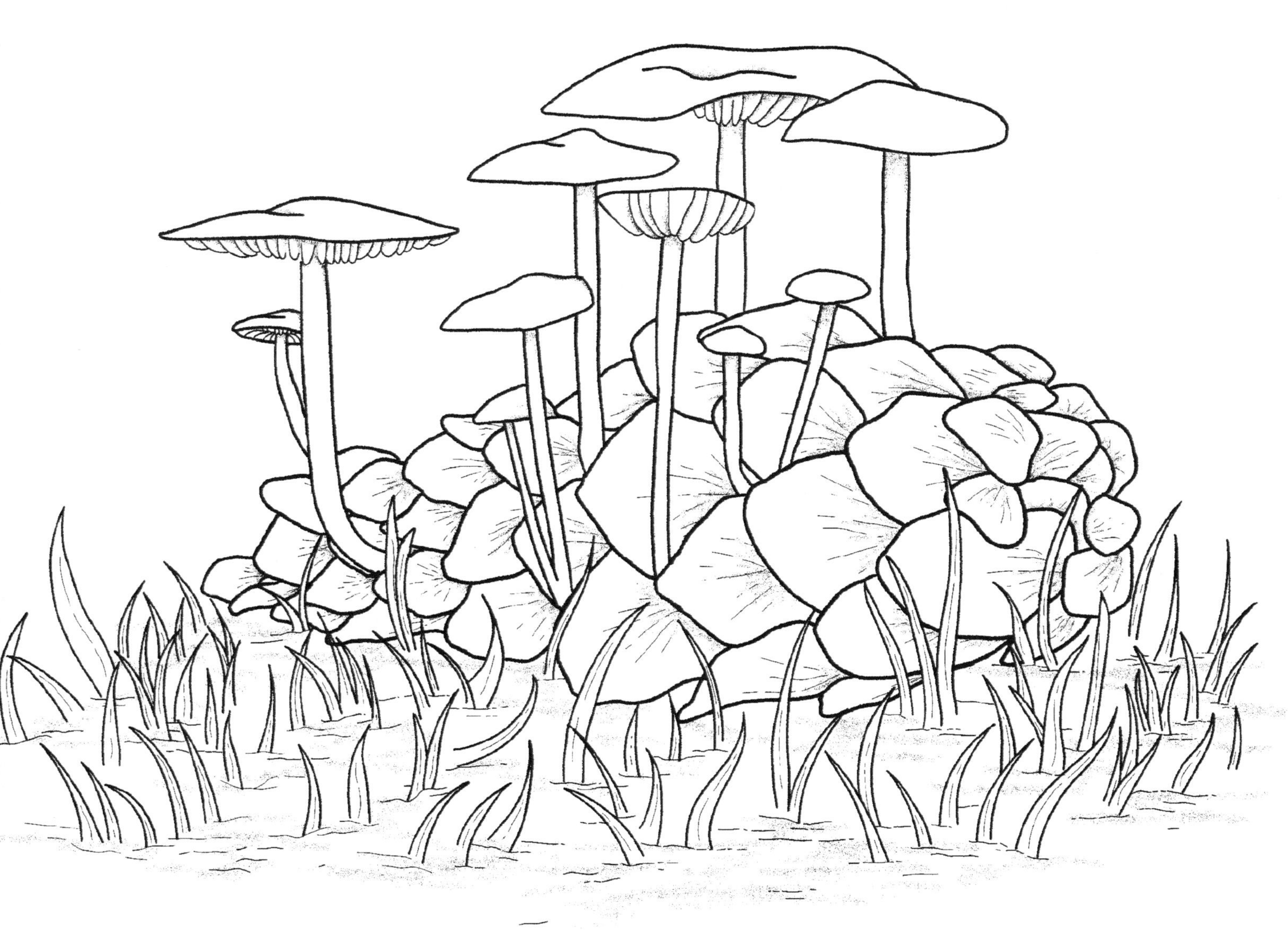

SCARLET BONNET

Mycena adonis

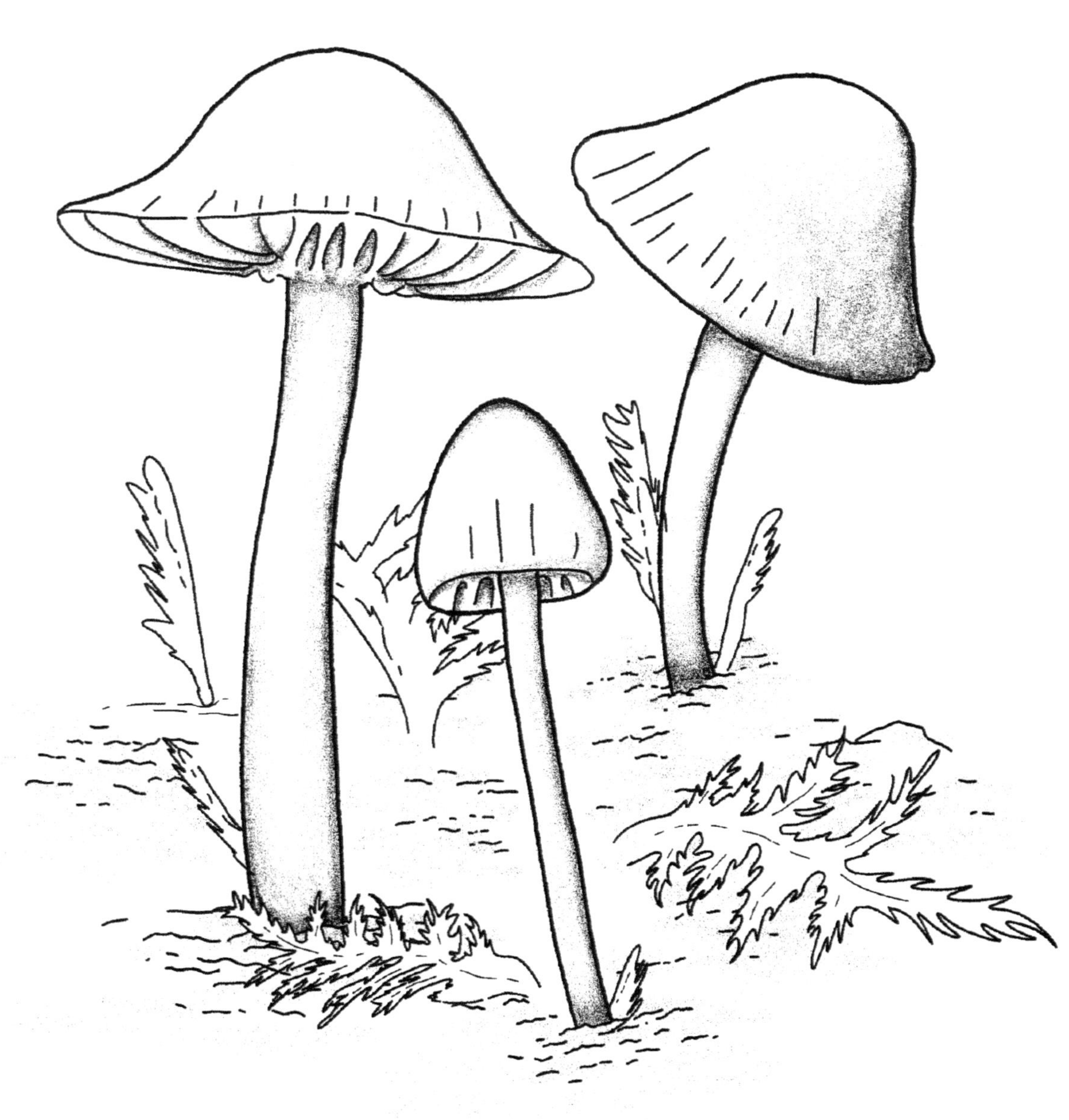

OYSTER
Pleurotus ostreatus

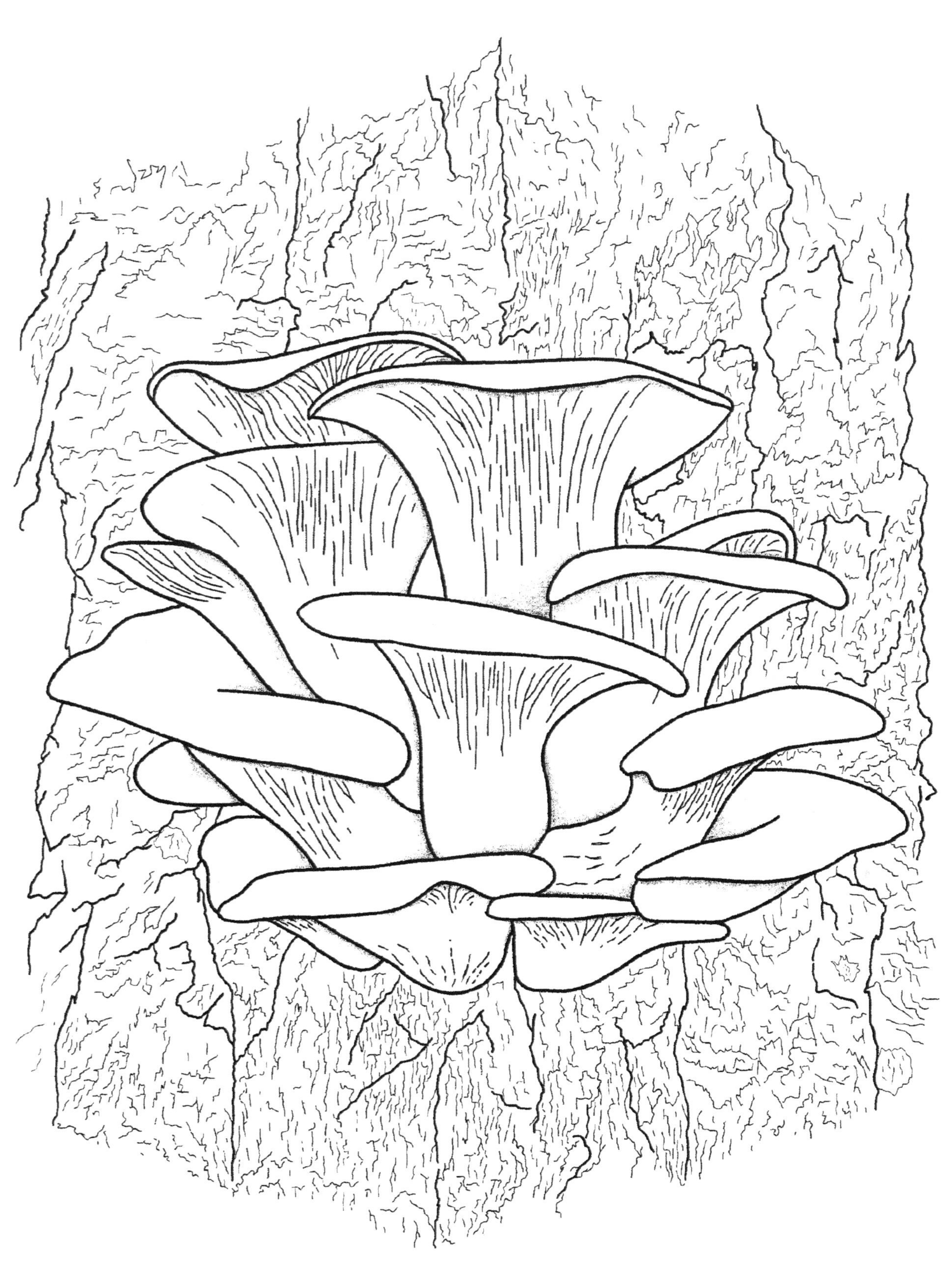

PARROT MUSHROOM

Gliophorus psittacinus

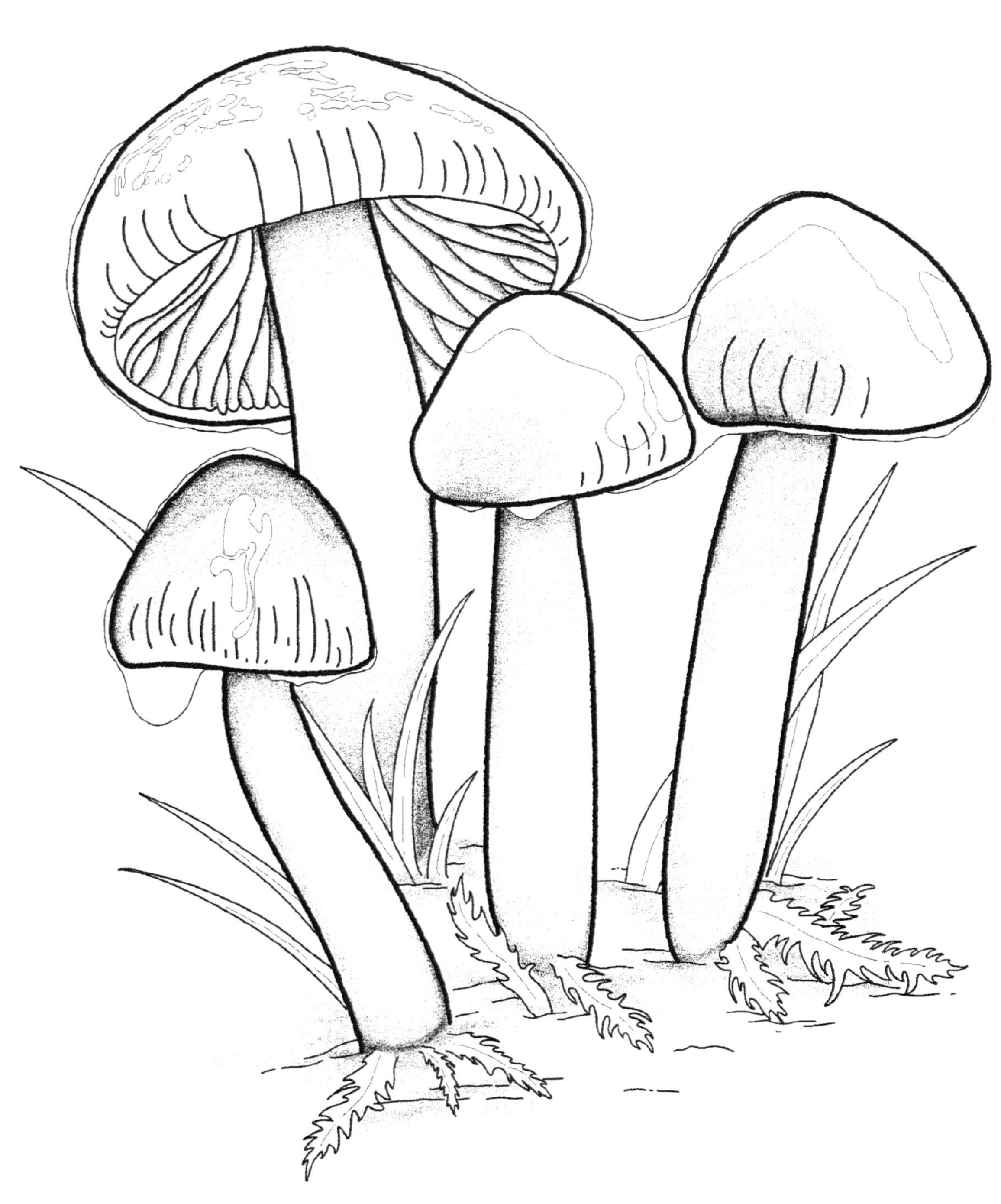

RED PINE

Lactarius deliciosus

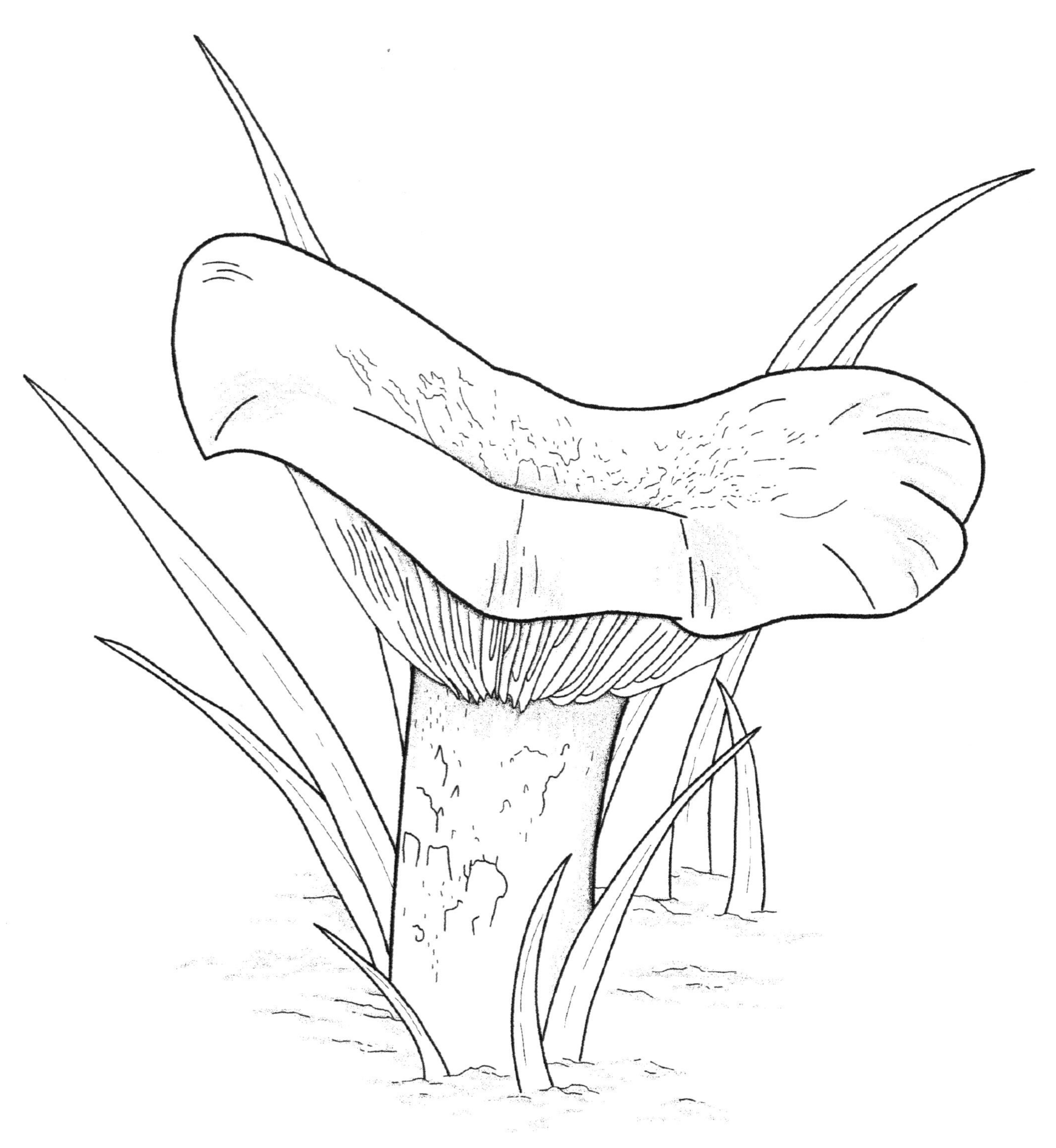

SHAGGY MANE
Coprinus comatus

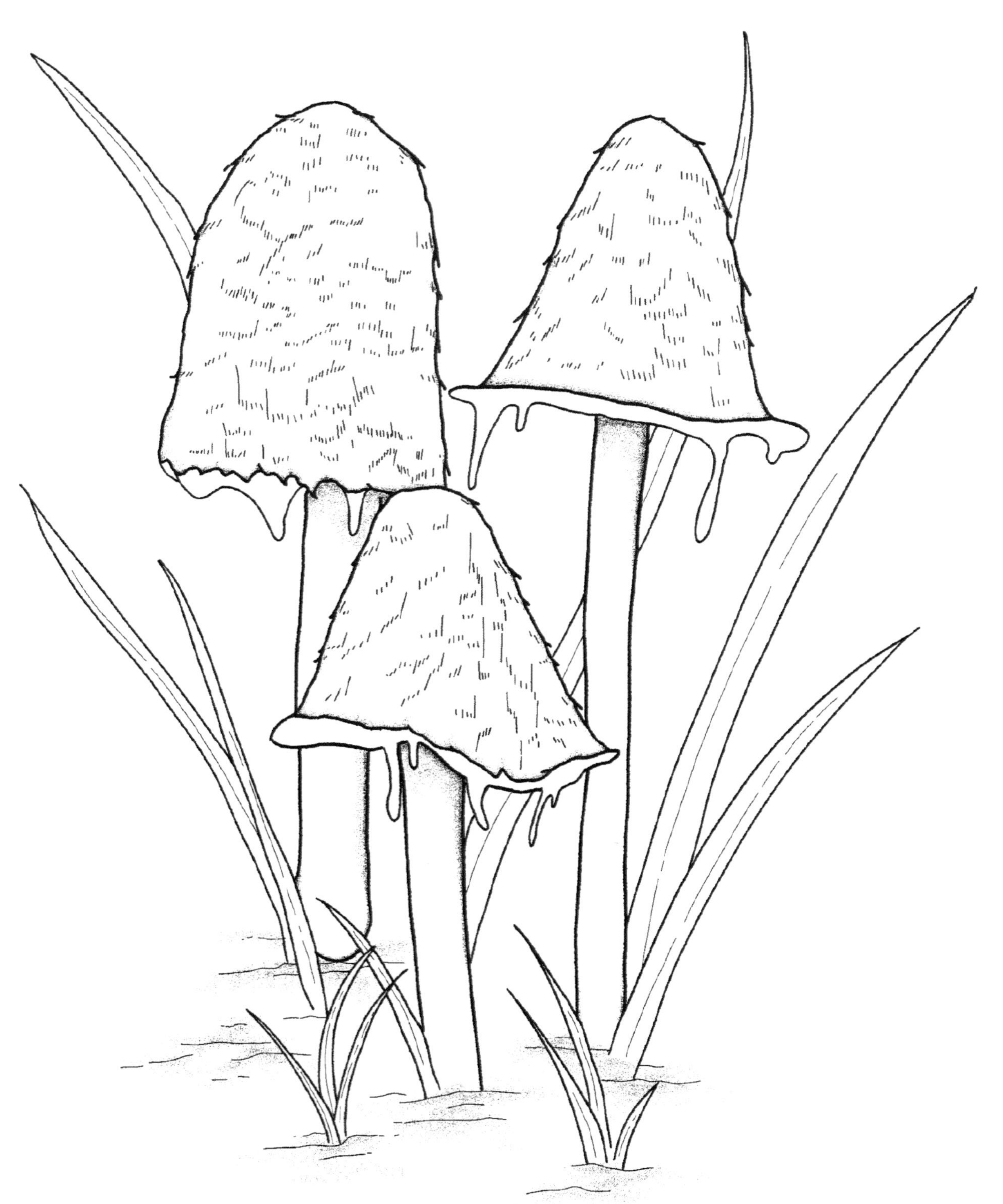

TWO COLORED BOLETE
Baorangia bicolor

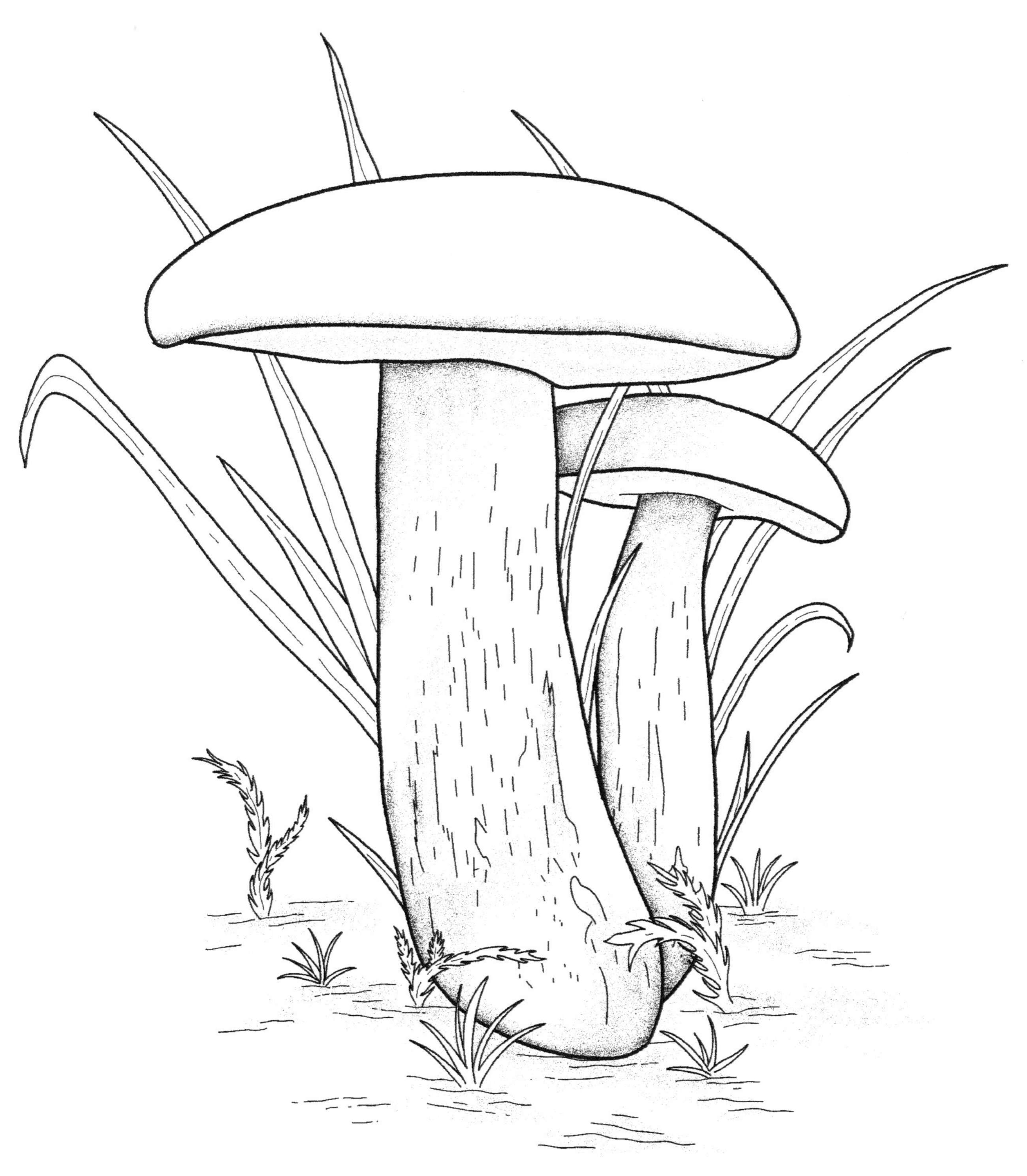

CHANTARELLE
Cantharellus

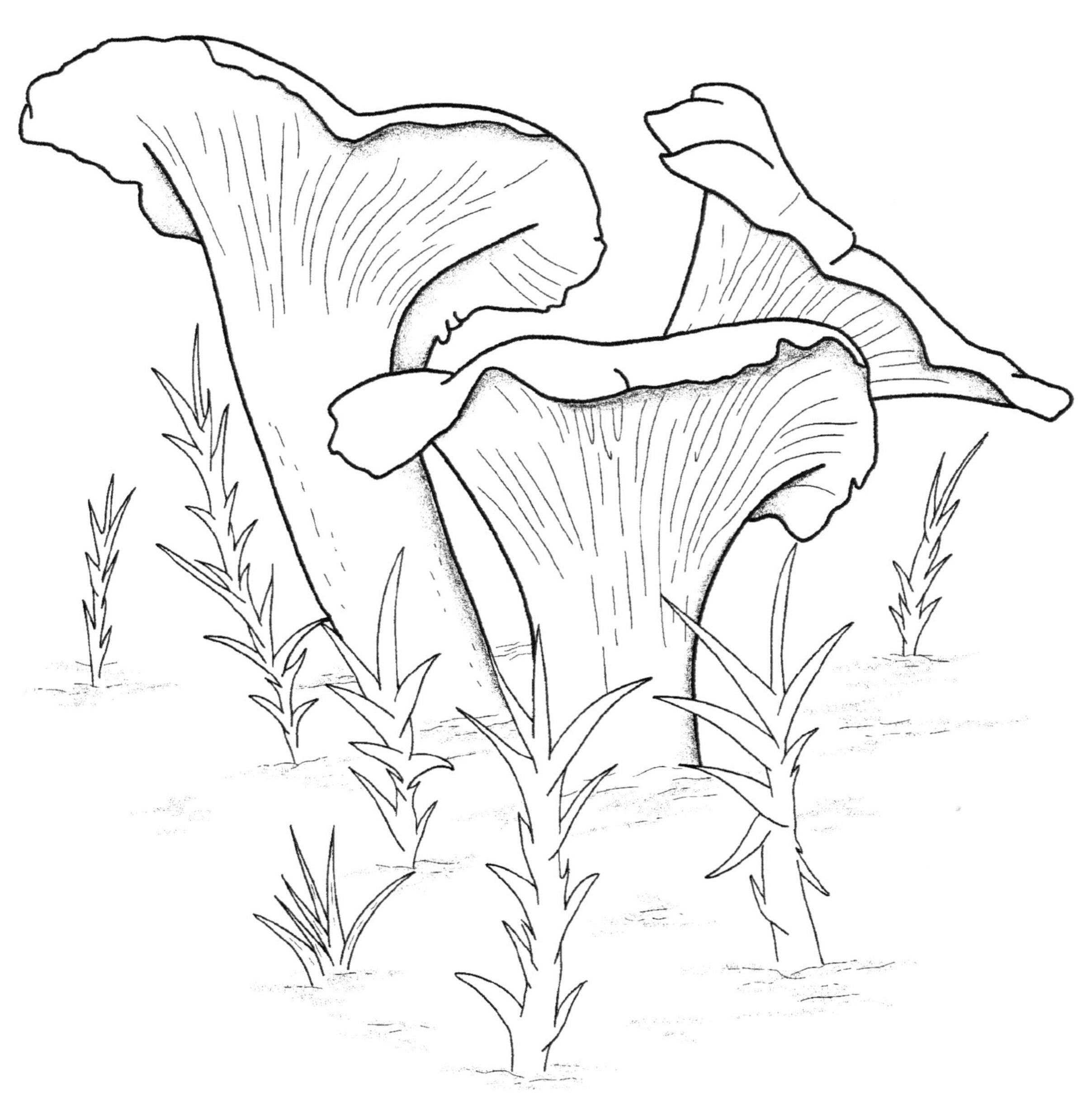

CRAB BRITTLEGILL

Russula xerampelina

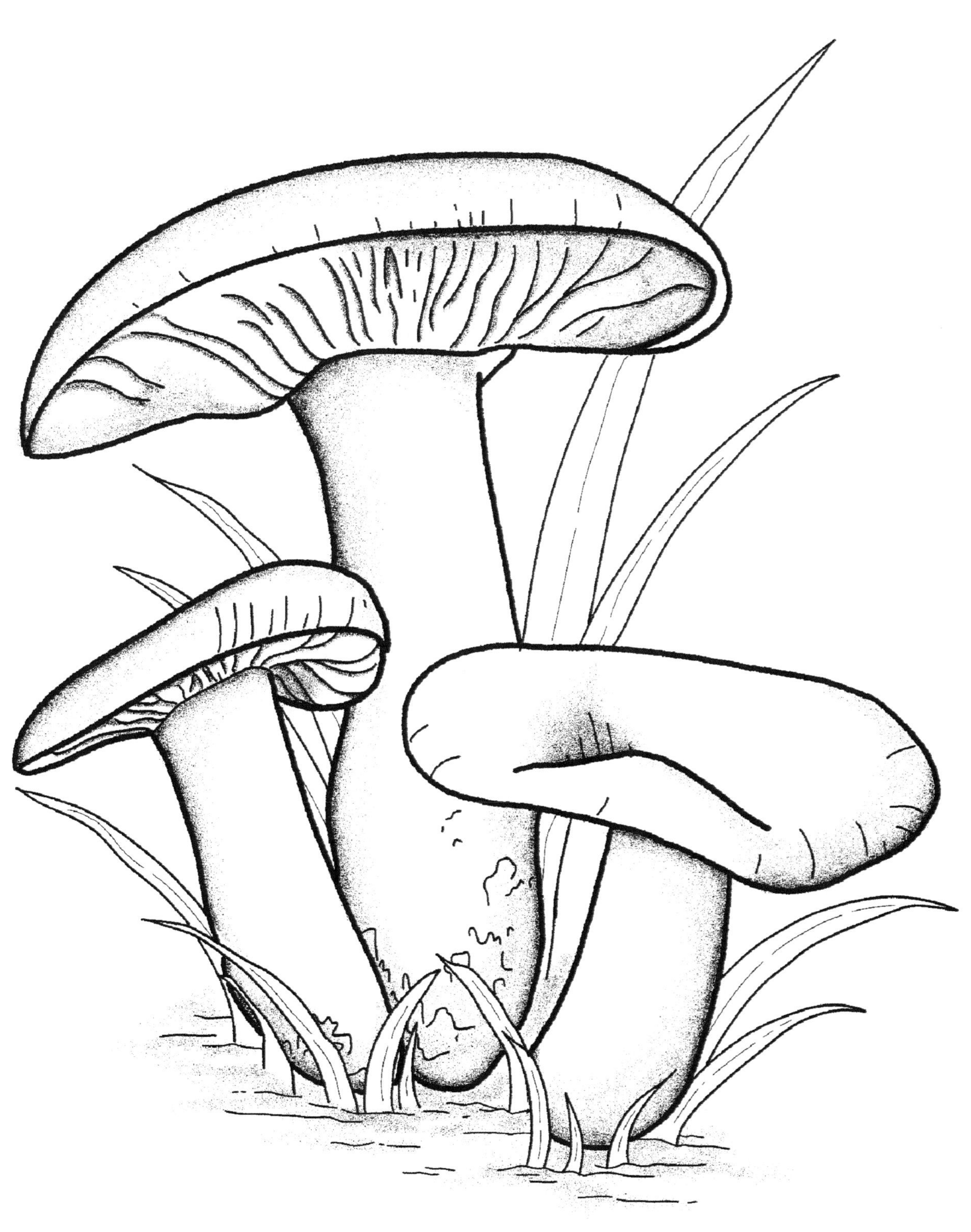

DEADLY SKULLCAP
Galerina marginata

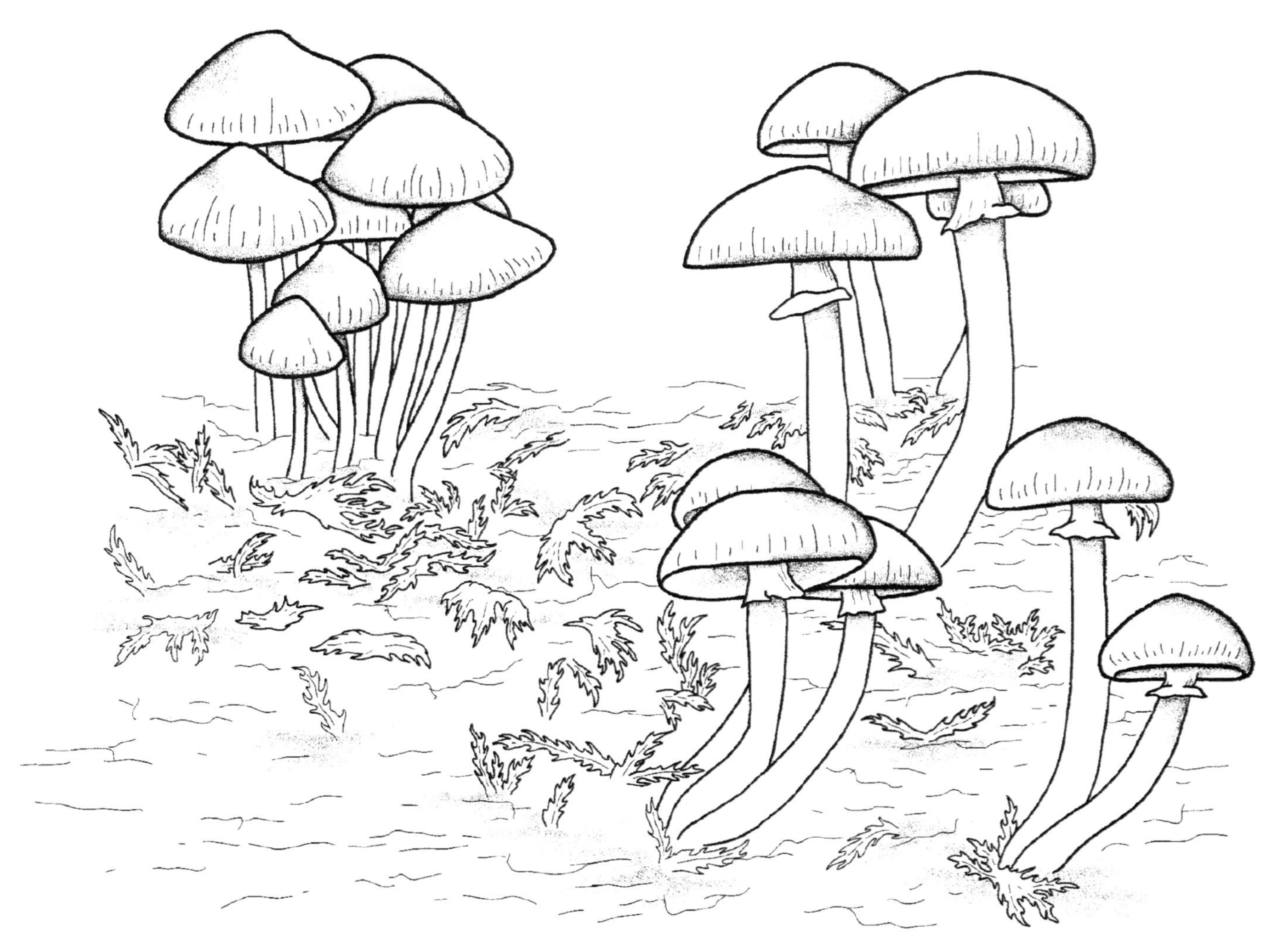

NETTED STINKHORN
Phallus duplicatus

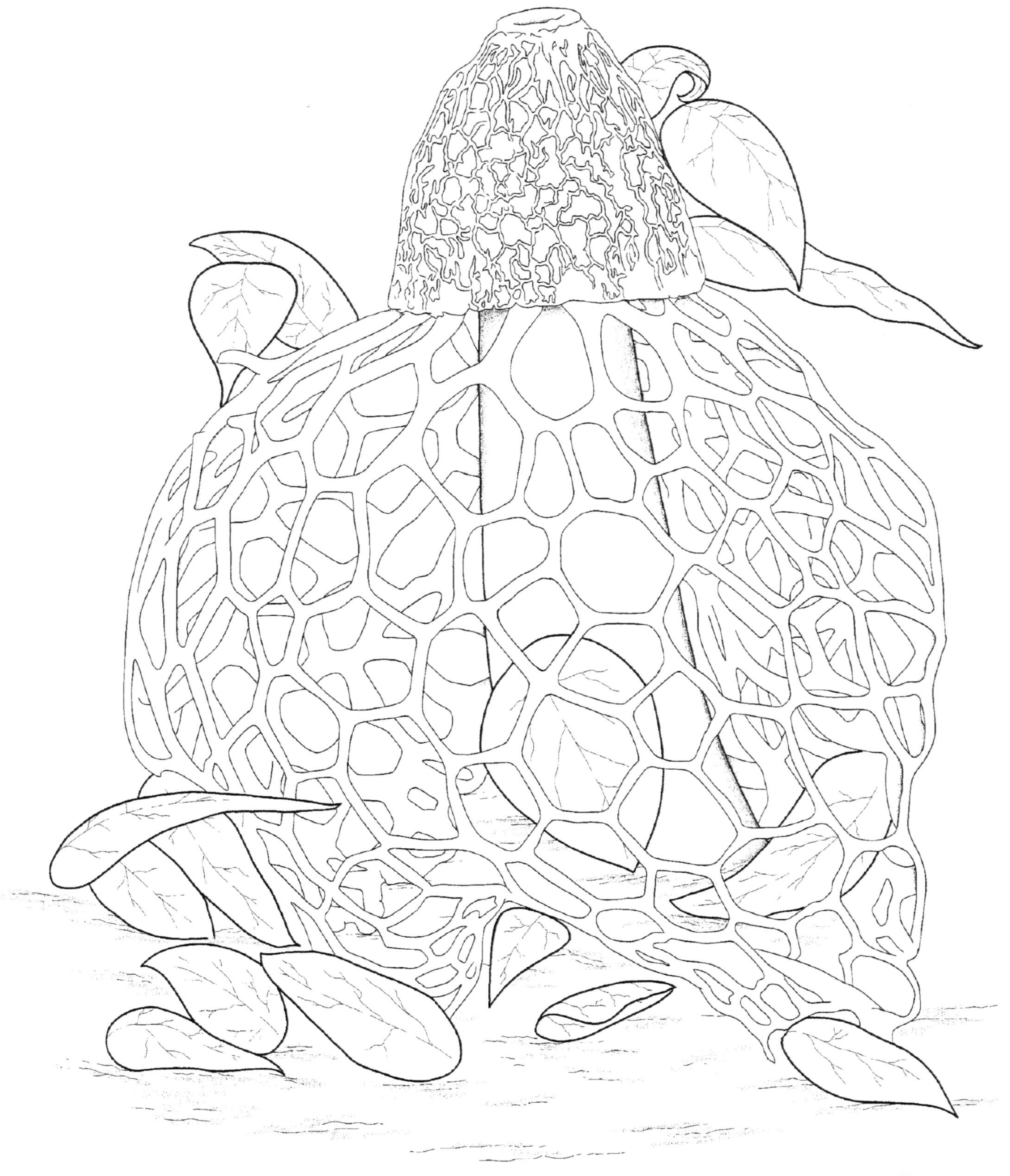

PIXIE'S PARASOL
Mycena interrupta

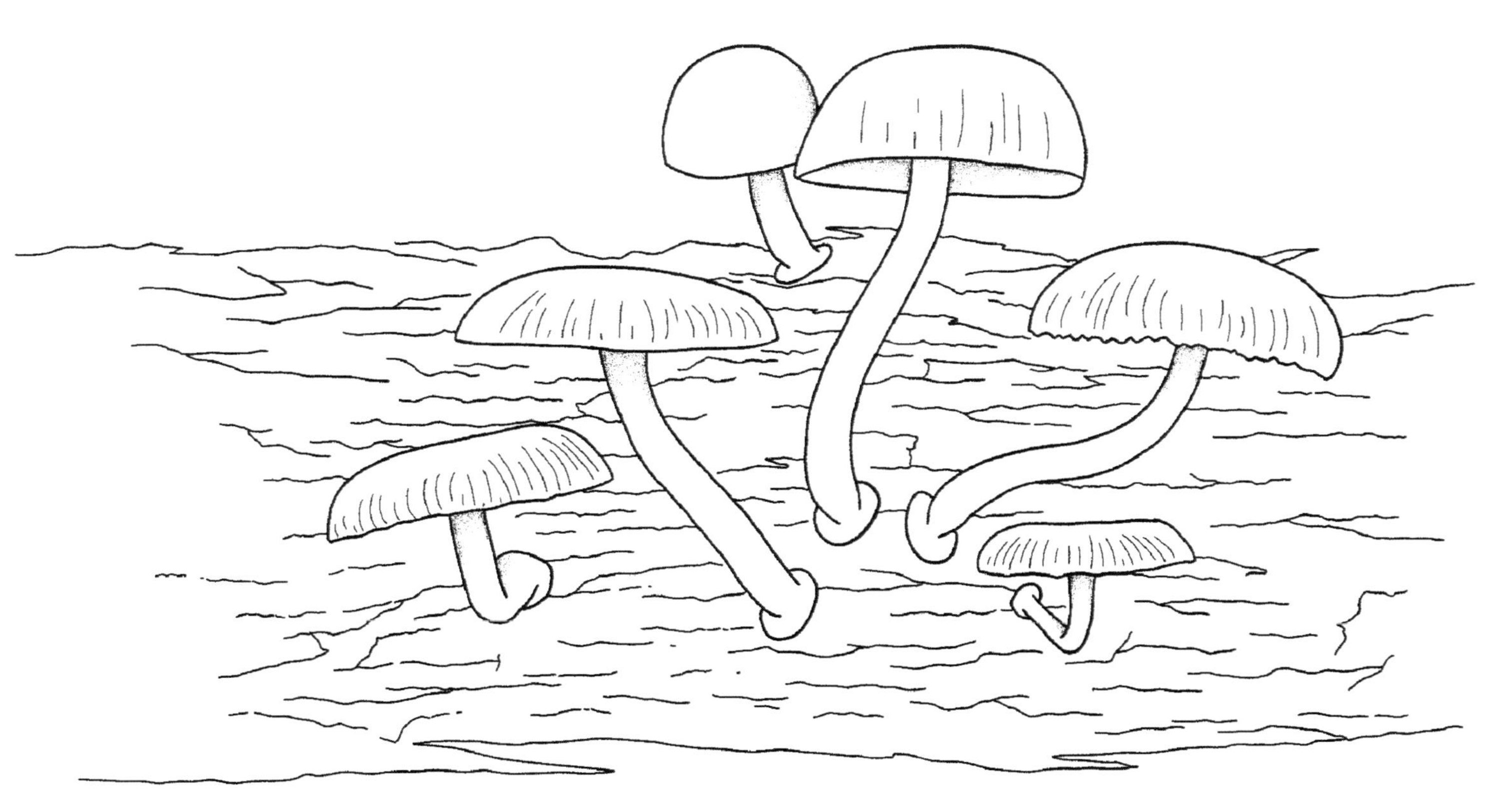

WORM CORAL

Clavaria fragilis

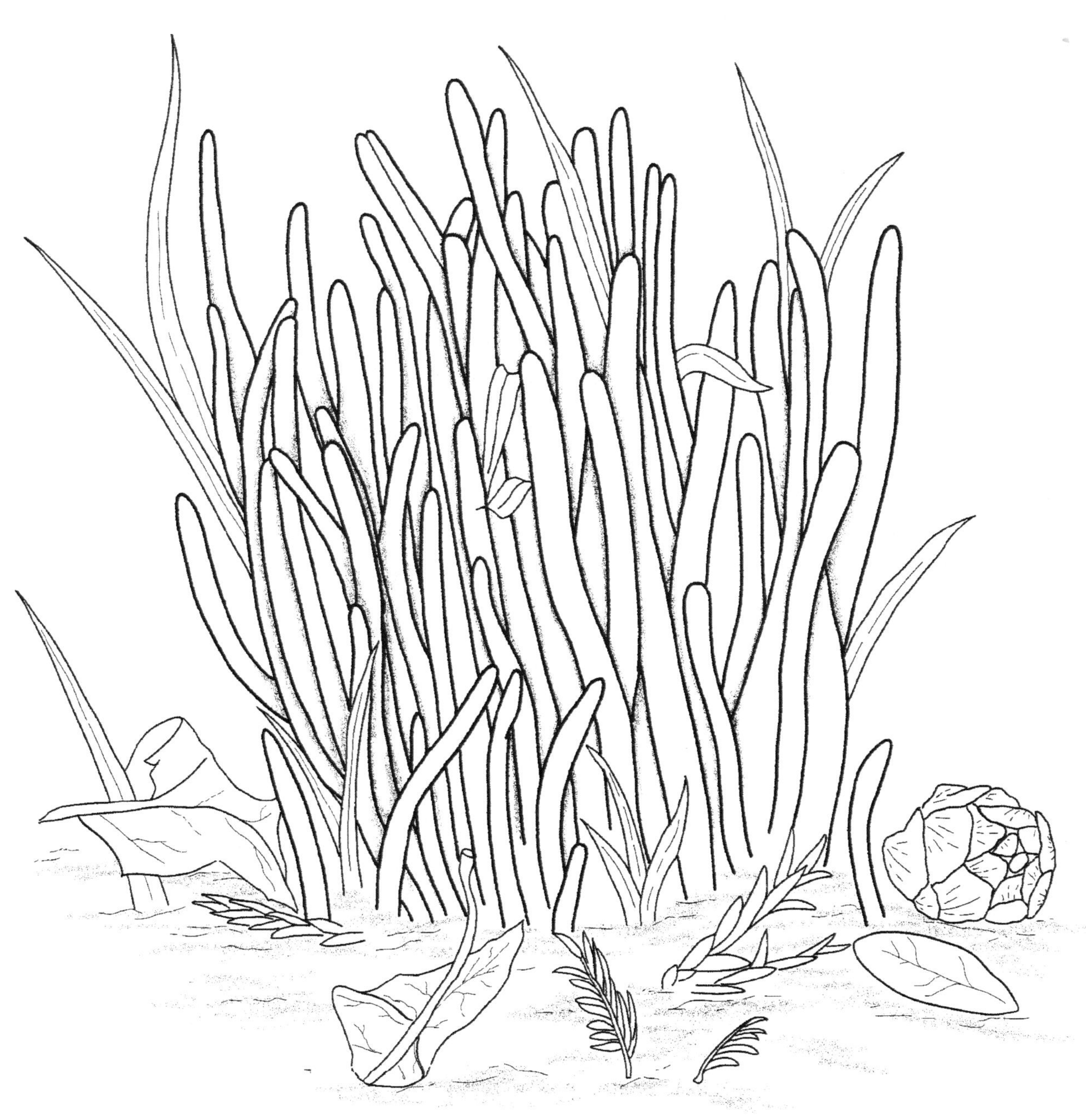

ROSY VEINCAP
Rhodotus palmatus

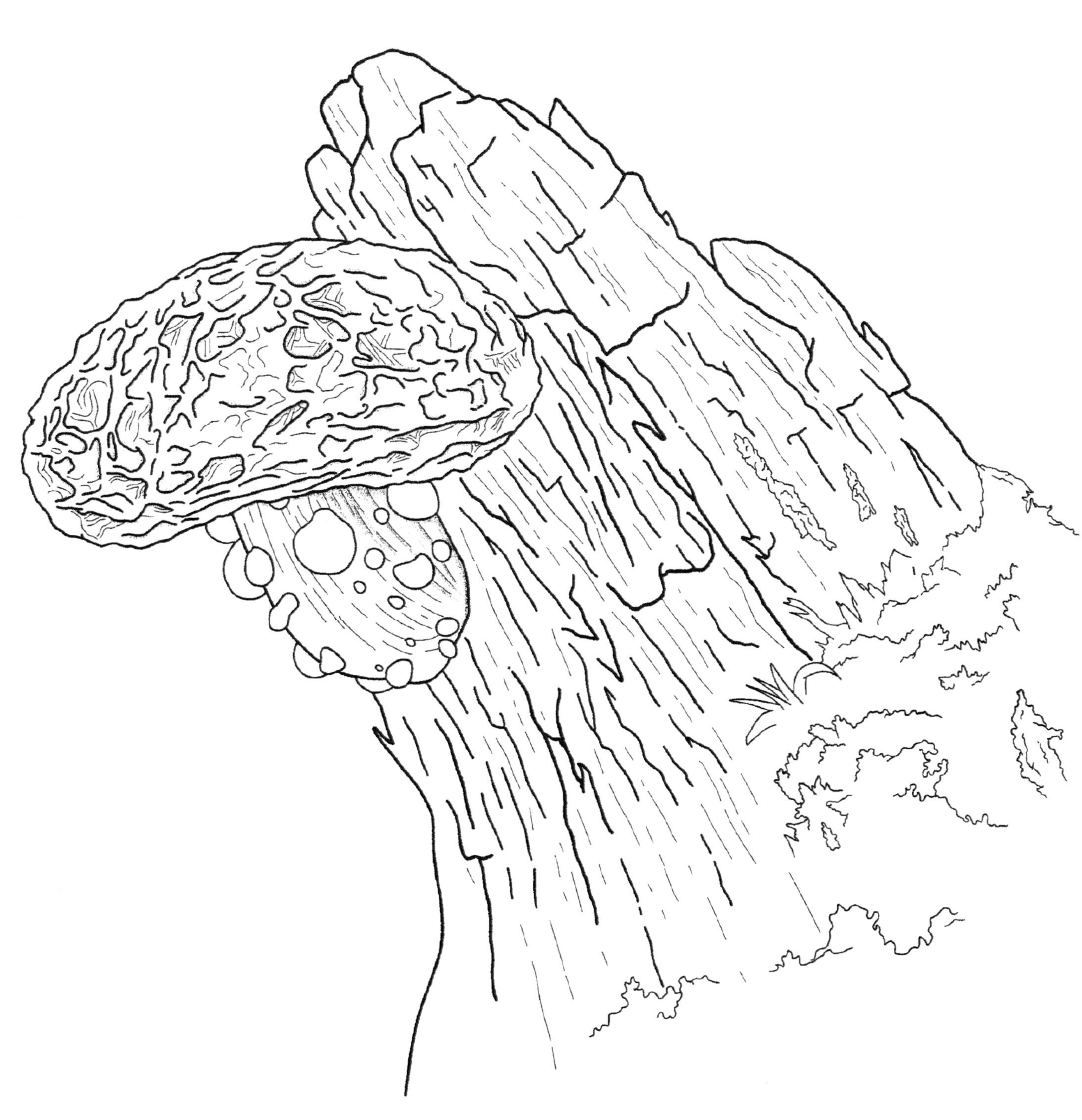

DEVILS CUP
Urnula craterium

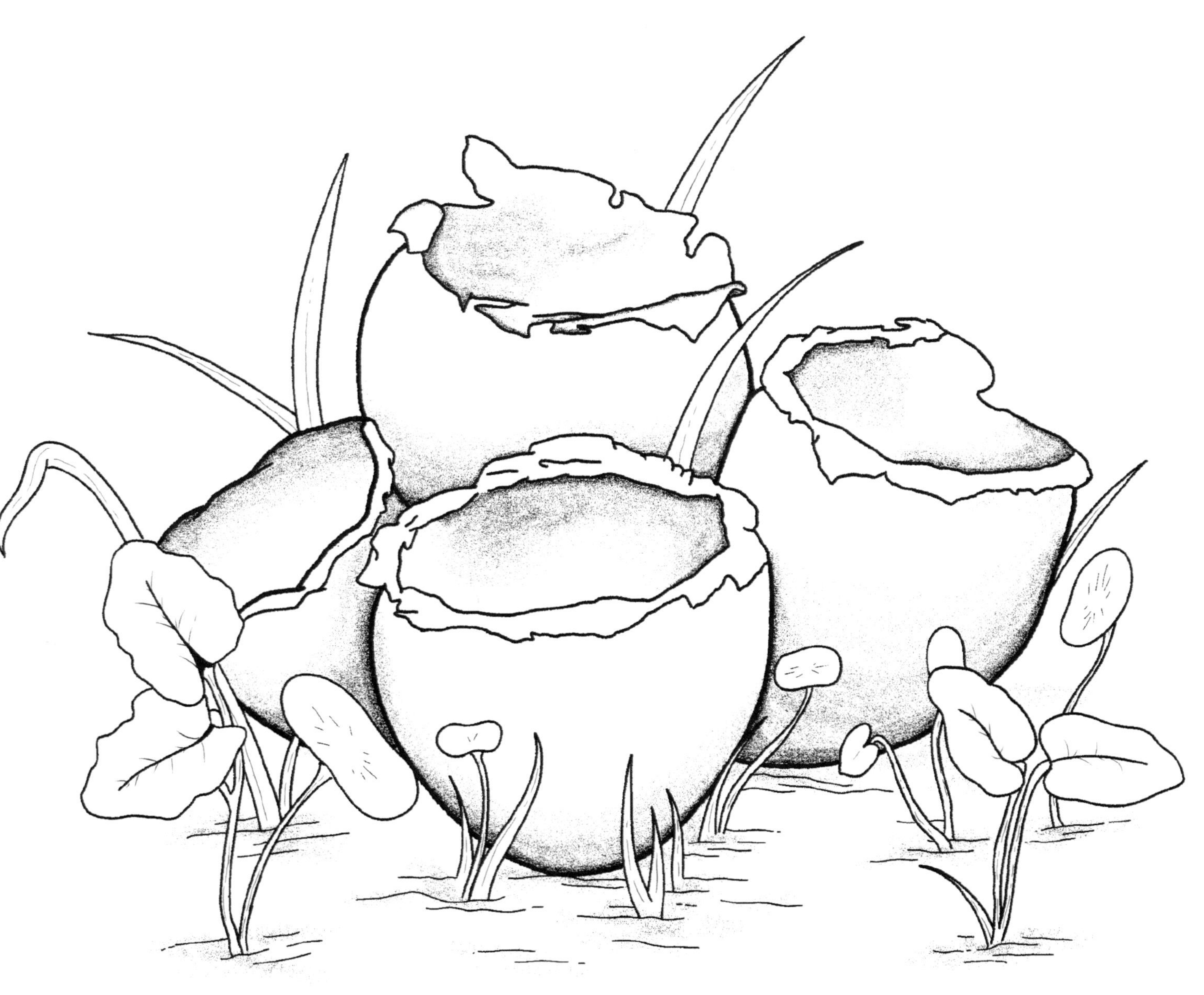

PLEATED INK CAP
Parasola plicatilis

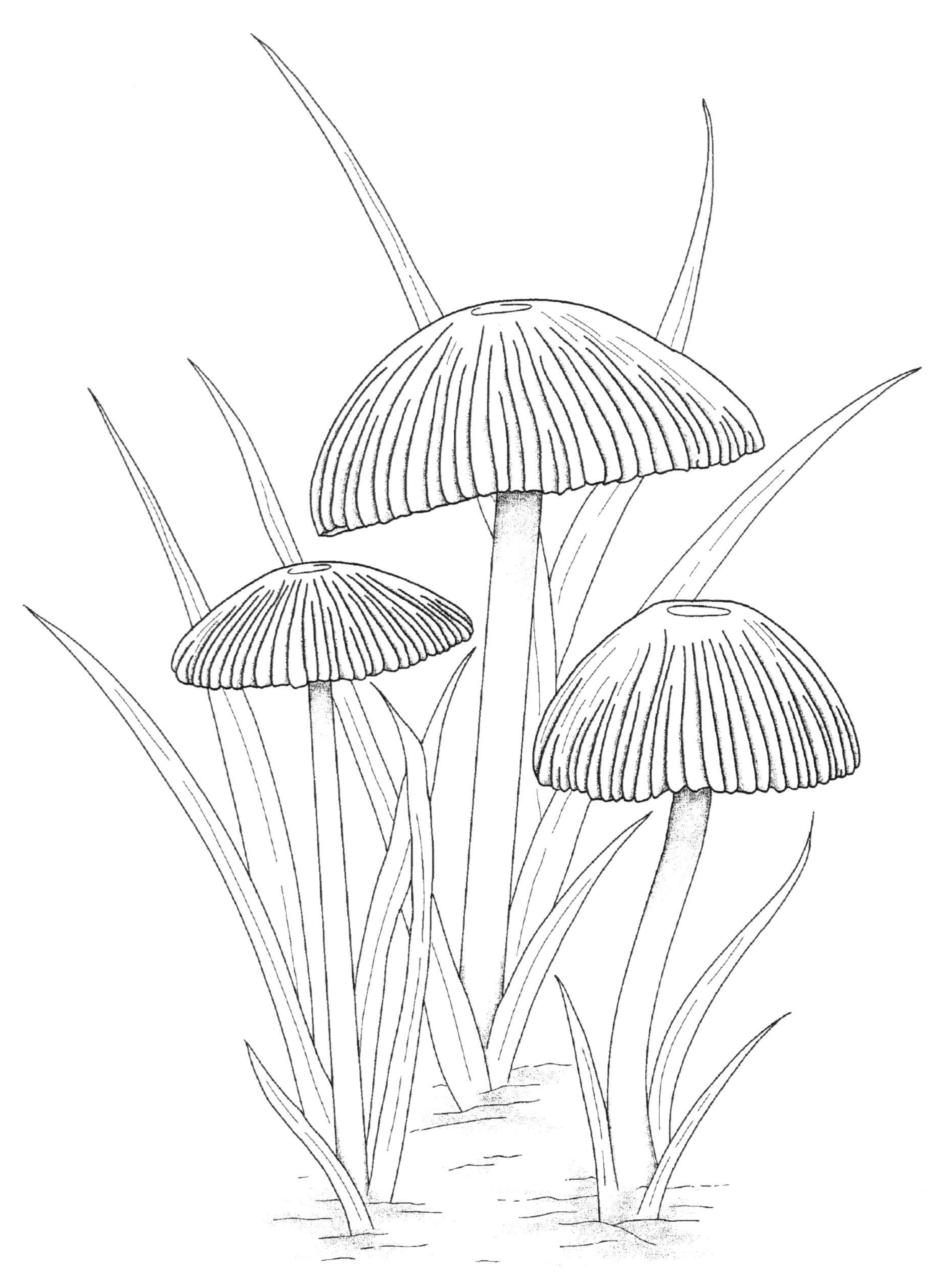

APRICOT JELLY
Guepinia helvelloides

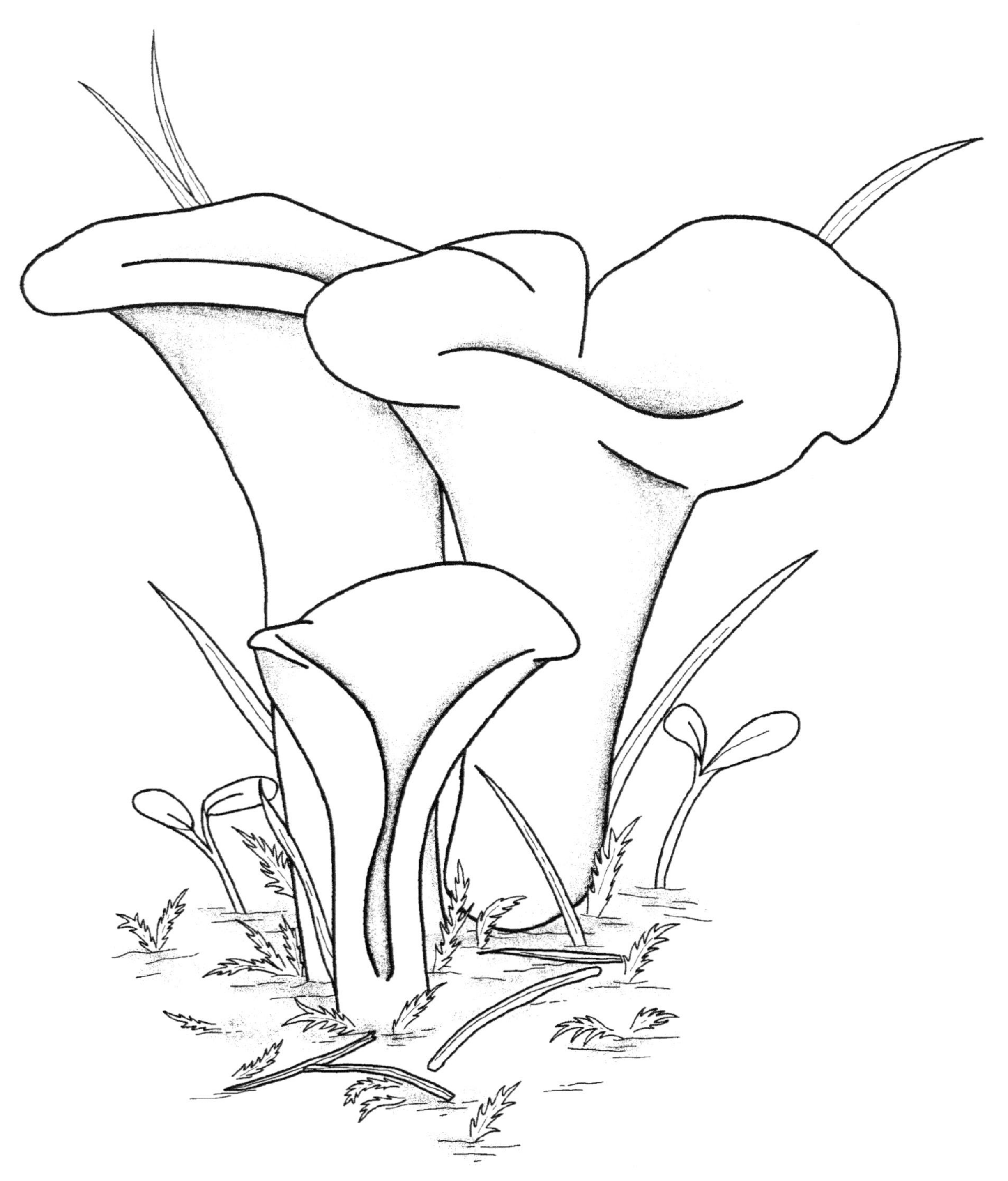

ENOKITAKE
flammulina velutipes

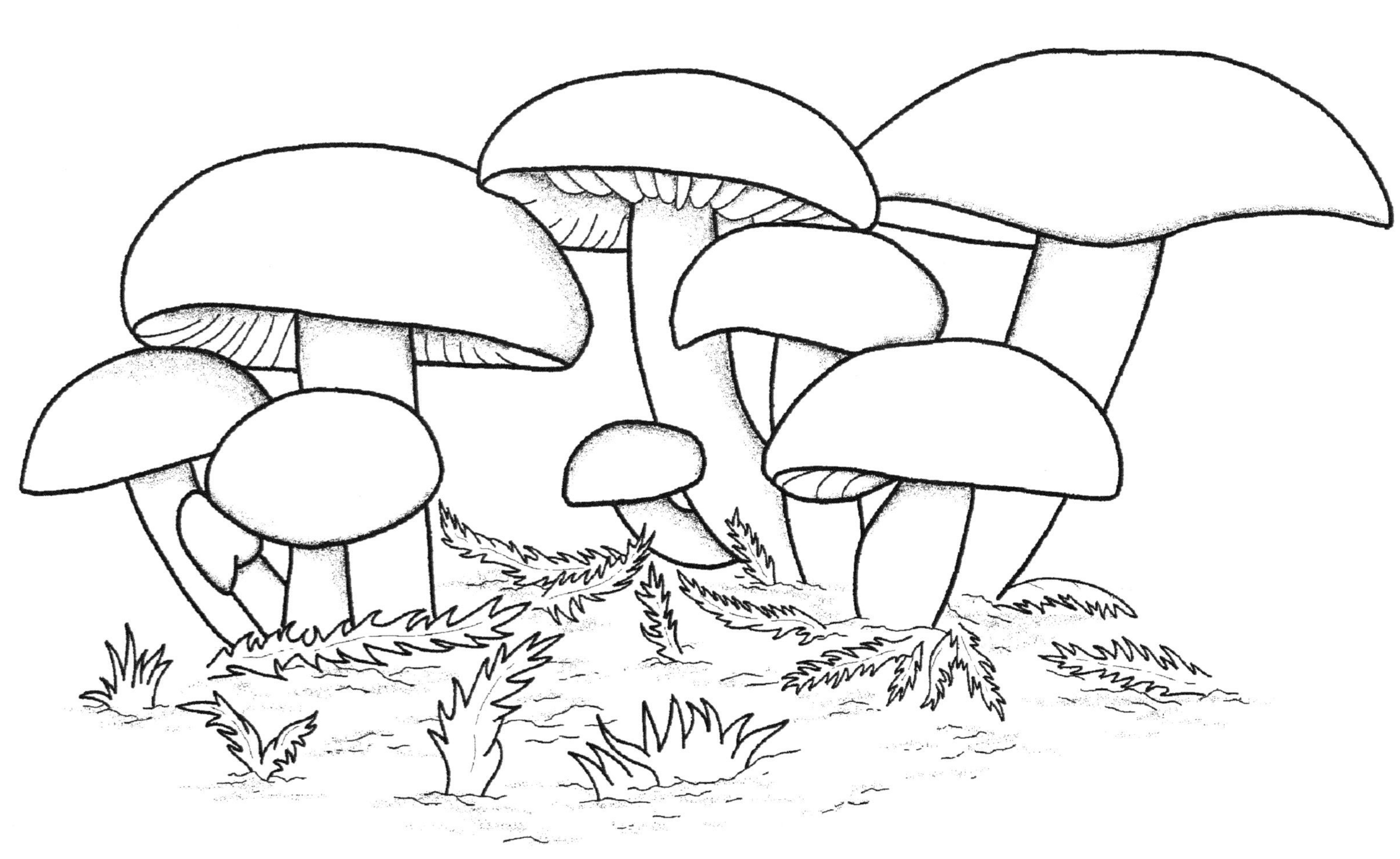

EARTH STAR
Geastrales

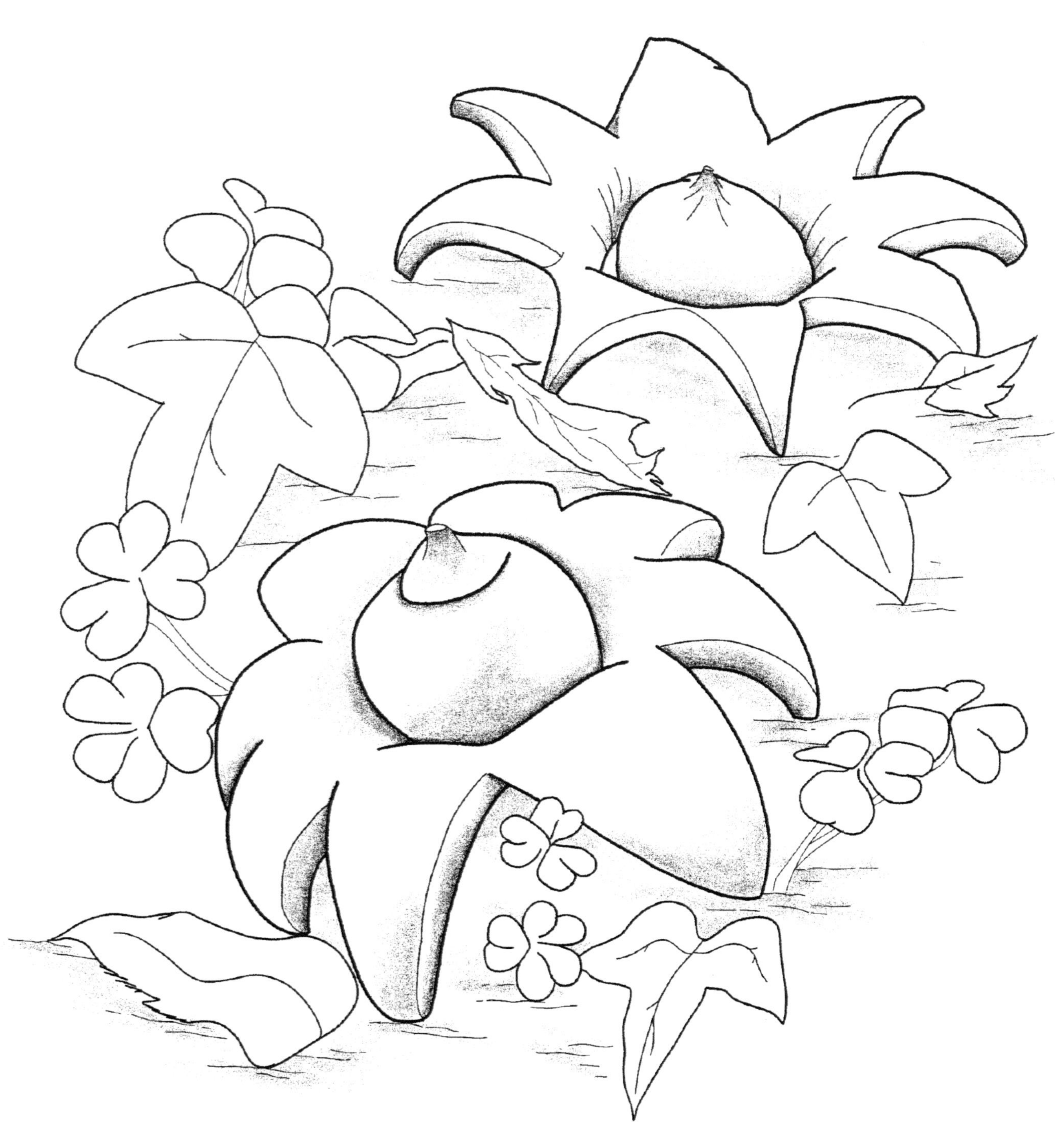